BEGINNING YOUR CAREER SEARCH

A Hands-on Approach to Building Your Career Portfolio

BEGINNING YOUR CAREER SEARCH

A Hands-on Approach to Building Your Career Portfolio

Fourth Edition

James S. O'Rourke, IV

University of Notre Dame

PEARSON

Prentice
Hall

Upper Saddle River, New Jersey 07458

VP/Editorial Director: Jeff Shelstad
Acquisitions Editor: David Parker
Project Development Manager: Ashley Santora
Associate Director Manufacturing: Vincent Scelta
Production Editor & Buyer: Wanda Rockwell
Printer/Binder: Bind-Rite Graphics

10 9 8 7 6 5 4 3 2 1
ISBN 0-13-172798-2

BEGINNING YOUR CAREER SEARCH

A Hands-on Approach to Building Your Career Portfolio

Fourth Edition

Table of Contents

DEDICATION

To those who matter most in my life: Pam, Colleen, Molly, and Kathleen. And, of course, Jay and Cianan. And to those who help to make my life intellectually interesting, socially meaningful, and fun each day, my colleagues: Sandra, Sondra, Carol and Cynthia. You guys are just the best.

A WORD OF ACKNOWLEDGMENT

To those Notre Dame students – graduate and undergraduate – who talked about this with me, gave me their insights, shared their frustrations and fears, and gladly let us print their resumes and correspondence. And to Karen Dowd, director of Career Services in the Mendoza College of Business at Notre Dame for her counsel and guidance. And, the one person without whom this simply wouldn't have happened, my assistant, Elisa Podrasky. Thanks to you each. You made this look easy.

INTRODUCTION

What This Book Is About

Beginning your career search can be a frightening, frustrating, and very stressful experience. Many college and university students, in spite of many years of study and thoughtful reflection, still aren't completely certain who they want to work for, want they want to do for a living, or even what they hope to be when they graduate. That's the bad news. The good news is that virtually everyone makes it through the career search experience healthy, sane, and fully-employed.

Transforming yourself from an aspiring student with career ambitions to a full-time professional with an employer, a regular paycheck, and some reasonable prospects for advancement isn't easy. You can do it, though. Literally millions of young men and women do each year.

This little book may be of some help. In here, you will find some straight-forward, practical advice on how to assemble a career portfolio, and how to write a resume that works. You will see what to avoid in your resume and how to correspond with a prospective employer. Employers take everything you write very seriously, so you should pay special attention to the section on introductory, cover letters and follow-up, thank-you letters.

Equally important is knowing who you want to work for (and why). This book contains some advice on researching the companies you most want to work for. This research will be especially helpful, not only in locating the ideal firm to begin your career with, but also during job interviews. Employers think it's particularly important for job applicants to know a great deal about the company *before* the interview process ever begins. This book will show you how to find that sort of information, and how to use it to your advantage during an interview.

You will also find helpful suggestions on how to conduct yourself during an interview: what to wear, what *not* to wear, what to bring with you, greeting an interviewer, nonverbal skills, and how to listen carefully to what's being said.

Hundreds of interviewers were asked what they're looking for in professional job candidates. The same interviewers were asked what turns them off when they're speaking with job applicants. You'll find their responses, along with a reasonably complete list of questions you should be prepared to answer. This book also talks about questions you do not have to answer, as well as questions you might want to ask your interviewer.

Specific suggestions on what to do *after* the interview are also here, along with an updated list of the reasons job interviews fail. You will find a thorough discussion of new interview techniques, including critical-incident or behavioral-based interviews. We'll also give you some ideas on how to negotiate with a company once you're offered a job.

If you're concerned about your writing skills, you will find sample letters of application and several follow-up, thank-you letters. These are authentic letters, written by business students just like you. Those same students have also agreed to share copies of their resumes. No matter what your academic or work background, you're likely to find samples that will help you draft that first letter and put together a resume that best represents your skills, experience and potential.

Assembling a Career Portfolio

You'll have a much better chance of defining and achieving your career goals, and a better chance of finding the ideal organization to take you where you want to go if you establish a Career Portfolio and update it periodically.

"What's in a Career Portfolio?" you might ask, and "Why exactly do I need one?" Most dictionaries define a portfolio simply as a "collection." In practical terms, a "folio" is a sheet folded once to make two leaves, and is used for carrying other papers, drawings or documents. The prefix "port" simply refers to portability – you can carry it with you. Many professionals collect portfolios of their work, including artists, architects, designers, writers, and others, to demonstrate their competence and creativity in their chosen fields.

Just as a professional photographer or writer might collect her best works, you should consider gathering together those documents which will portray your performance, experience, and potential in the best possible light. And, once assembled, your Career Portfolio will help you to periodically reassess your career ambitions and professional direction, as well as the need for additional education, training, or experience.

To answer your first question about what a Career Portfolio contains, you should know that no two are exactly the same, but most contain similar documents, including a personal statement, a resume, a cover letter, a list of references, samples of your writing or professional accomplishments, and a follow-up thank-you letter.

Even if you're a year or more away from graduation, the best time to get started on your career search is right now. After all, the sooner you get started, the better your resume will look, the greater the list of potential employers, and the better your chances will be. Remember, your professors, friends, and family are all pulling for you and will likely be a great help as you begin to think about your career. But writing that resume, drafting those letters, and finding just the right employer is up to you.

Good luck with your search and best wishes as you embark on a new career.

J. S. O'Rourke, IV
The Eugene D. Fanning Center
Mendoza College of Business
University of Notre Dame

CHAPTER 1

ASSESSING YOURSELF

A successful entrepreneur from Chicago was speaking to a small group of college students not long ago about their career ambitions. The students all wanted to know how he had become so successful and how they, in turn, could succeed in business. "You have to have dreams," he said. "You've got to have some definable objectives that you can aspire to. Ambition will carry you just so far," he added, "but you must first know where you're going."

One student said that she hoped to run her own business one day, while another aspired to become a broker on Wall Street. A third said that he hoped to establish a charitable foundation for children. "Great ideas," the entrepreneur responded. "All noble ambitions." He paused for a moment and said, "Now, how do you plan to get there?" The students were puzzled. They had thought, based on the title of his talk, that he would provide them with advice, perhaps a plan for achieving their goals.

"I thought you might help us with that," replied one student. "I'm happy to do that," he said. "Here's the advice: identify your goals, define the skills and competencies needed to achieve them, find or start an organization that will help you get there. Then, surround yourself with people who share your goals and whose ambitions are the same as your own. Finally, make sure that what you're doing has some redeeming social value. Give back to the community and to those who helped you succeed."

"Sounds simple," said one skeptical student. "But exactly how do we get started?"

"The path to success," the entrepreneur replied, "begins with self-assessment. You must first know who you are in order to find a path to who you want to become."

Daydreaming as a Way of Identifying Your Goals

We all have dreams, ambitions, and objectives in life. Some are vague, fuzzy notions about being wealthy or successful. Others have a more tangible look to them: a specific kind of car, a house in a nice neighborhood, fashionable clothes, or a particular set of professional skills. Much of this is daydreaming – an imaginative exercise that lets us wander through places we have never been, with people we have never met. Adults sometimes scold young people about daydreaming, saying it's unproductive and useless. "Be practical," they say. "Make something of yourself." But even adults daydream.

Some of you may have many years of work experience or may have raised a family before returning to school. The very fact that you can imagine a goal – a new job, a different career, or personal independence – means that personal growth and improvement are possible for you. As the artist Pablo Picasso once said, "Anything you can imagine is real." Surprisingly, daydreaming can be useful. You must learn to harness the energy and imagination involved in those dreams and turn them into specific, well-defined, attainable goals.

First, answer a few questions for yourself. What do you want out of life? What do you hope to become? Aside from the usual material possessions most people have, what else do you want? What contributions do you hope to make to the world? When your life has been lived, what would you like to be remembered for? What will you have done that will make a difference in business, in your country, your city, or your neighborhood? And, equally important, how do you plan to go about it? How will you get there? What will you do to make those dreams come true?

Next, set priorities and limits as you establish your goals. What's most important to you? What comes first? Your family? An education? Seeing the world? If two or more of these values come into conflict – say, an opportunity to manage an office overseas conflicts with a desire to have your oldest child complete high school in one location – how will you handle that? You should be clear about your priorities and establish limits on what you are willing to do to achieve your goals and what you are not willing to do. This process will be challenging, of course, because many of your priorities in life will change with time; as you grow older, different objectives take on greater importance. Keep in mind that career planning is a continuous process and your definition of a career will undoubtedly change as you grow older and move through various stages of life.

Finally, ask yourself what's reasonable. Career goals, as well as job goals, should be reasonable, reachable, and rational. Don't set yourself up for disappointment or failure. To make your career goals reachable and to establish a job search program that will succeed, you will want to consider a personal profile.

Developing a Personal Profile

Socrates said, "Know thyself," and Shakespeare said "unto thine ownself be true." They were both right. They may not have had a job search in mind as they wrote those words – perhaps they did. Who knows? But they did pinpoint an essential element of career planning and employment communication: self-knowledge. Unless you know who you are, you'll never be able to sell yourself to an employer. Every good sales rep knows the product line and, in this case, the product is you, your skills, and your potential.

A personal profile is the picture of you that emerges after some careful thought and honest response to a few personal questions. The Personal Profile and Career Planning Guide in this chapter were developed by Richard Huether, a former marketing executive at General Electric Corporation. This brief, simple device, which has been used successfully by thousands

2

of college students, may prove useful in assessing your prospects for employment. Take a few minutes to answer these questions and you should have the foundations of a career search and resume.

The Role of Your Personal Profile and Career Planning Guide

The role of this guide is to help you make better career decisions and to manage the available resources to reach this decision. It is designed as a working document that is adjusted regularly, not simply a one-time exercise. If you begin using the guide now, it will not only help to reduce confusion and frustration in setting your career goals, but will also assist in charting a path to reaching them.

Developing Your Career Planning Guide

Step 1: Complete the "Profile" section under *Personal Inventory*, including a two-line description of who you are.

Step 2: List your greatest "Skills and Strengths." For instance: strong debater, well organized, accomplished leader, good in mathematics, competent writer, and so on.

Step 3: Fill in the title of the "Targeted Position" that would be most appealing to you immediately after graduation under *Career Plan*.

TEST: How does your current list of skills and strengths generally match those you believe are needed for the job you've selected? If you see that critical skills are lacking or that the job doesn't call for your strongest assets, you might want to rethink the job you've selected. Don't underestimate what you already know about yourself and your ability to match that knowledge to a career.

Step 4: Complete the "Accomplished" section under *Activity/Work Experiences*. This column should be a natural outgrowth of your skills and strengths. Reach back to earlier in your college career, work experience, and even high school days to build this list. Work, school, church, and other experiences form the basis for this list. Clubs, sports, class projects, and part-time jobs could be included.

Step 5: Fill in the "Completed" column under *Academic Courses*. Here, list the courses that were most appealing to you and/or where you seem to have done your best work.

TEST: How did the two lists completed in Steps 4 and 5 use or support your "Skills and Strengths" listed in Step 2? Have you tried to expand on your strongest skills and strengths, either through outside activities or courses?

Remember, the quality of your career decision will be directly related to how well you use your strengths. Make sure you give these strengths a chance to grow and develop, either through academic or extra-curricular activities.

TEST: How did the two lists completed in Steps 4 and 5 support your choice for your first job in Step 3? If your "Completed" *Academic Courses* and *Activity/ Work Experiences* have little in common with this job, you may want to strongly consider a different choice. Either you need to re-evaluate your first job choice, or make plans to re-direct your curricular and extra-curricular activities to be more supportive of your choice.

Step 6: Fill in the title of the job that would be most appealing to you *five years after graduation* or five years from now; review the test that follows Step 3.

Step 7: Complete your *Career Plan* goal, keeping in mind what you have been saying about yourself in Steps 1 through 6. Don't be concerned if what you write down doesn't match what others have told you. No one can know you as well as you know yourself; through this process you will learn about your career goals from *you*, not from someone else.

Step 8: Complete the "Planned" column under *Academic Courses*. Look at the courses you have already taken and your accomplished *Activity/Work Experience*. Ask yourself what additional courses the University offers that would help you reach your career goal. Those choices, combined with this planning guide, should become the foundation of your next meeting (and all future meetings) with your academic advisor as you begin to take greater ownership of your education.

Step 9: Complete "Planned" *Activity and Work Experiences*. Using all the information you entered under *Academic Courses* and *Activity/Work Experience*, evaluate what extracurricular activities or jobs (i.e., internships or summer jobs) might enhance this plan by filling in blank spots in your experience or simulating actual working conditions.

TEST: The final and most important test is how well this process fits you. Look at your career goal. Does the combination of *Academic Courses* and *Work Experience* logically lead to this goal? And, is your *Career Plan* a logical extension of the person you know yourself to be, as described in your *Personal Inventory*? If the answers are yes, congratulate yourself! Remember, though, this is a working document. To help it serve you best, you should update it regularly. If the answer to either of these questions is *no*, you should review the process because you probably *didn't listen to yourself carefully.*

Using Your Personal Profile and Career Planning Guide

With Yourself. The guide is designed to create a working plan to get you from where you are now to where you want to be. It should be updated as "Planned" becomes "Completed" or "Accomplished." And you should review it as you grow both personally and professionally. Use it to record what you are saying to yourself about your ambitions, achievements, and your career goals.

With Advisors. Share it with your professors, academic advisors, and workplace supervisors. They can be a great source of ideas on how to enrich the process. Share it with friends you respect. Sometimes they can see things about you or changes in you that you have missed. Share it with your family to elicit their understanding and ideas. You will most likely find that they will take great pride in how you are approaching your career decision.

With Interviewers. This is really a "living" resume. For employment during college, it can reinforce your commitment to the position for which you are applying. For job interviews, it demonstrates your commitment to the opportunity the interview offers and to the plan that got you there.

Classroom Projects

1. Select four or five friends who know you relatively well. Ask each one to think for a day or so about your best quality as an individual. Tell them that you are developing a personal profile to accompany your career development plans and you are especially interested in knowing what they see as your strongest personal quality. Think carefully about their responses for another day or so before reacting. When you are ready, compose a brief paper that describes your best personal quality. Illustrate your paper with specific anecdotes, stories, and examples of how that quality plays a role in your life. Conclude your essay with a paragraph explaining how that personal quality might be put to work in a career.

2. Develop a set of goals for yourself. Before you begin writing, spend some time alone thinking about what you *really* want to do with your life. Think about those activities, pursuits, dreams, and ambitions that excite you the most. How would you like to spend your days? What sort of occupation, profession, or calling would give you the most satisfaction in life? After you've spent some time thinking about this, make a list of no more than ten important goals. When you have drawn up your list, re-write the list *in order of priority*. That is, your most important goal would come first, your second most important goal next, and so on.

3. Write a letter to an officer in a company you would most like to work for. Introduce yourself and explain why your ambitions, experience, and education – limited though they may be – are exactly what that company is looking for.

4. Develop a Personal Profile for yourself. Spend some time thinking about those things you do especially well, along with those activities you're not as good at doing. Think about what you like to do most or are best at. What do you like to do the least? What kinds of activities do you avoid whenever you can? Begin with a notepad, listing in any order they come to mind, those things you are skilled at or find easy to do. Write down those activities you can do best, especially if you can do them better than most people. Later group them together and see if you can fit them into categories, such as physical skills, interpersonal skills, quantitative abilities, verbal abilities, and so on. Next, list those things you can't do or aren't very good at. Be realistic about your abilities. Not everyone is good at everything they try. Concentrate on those things that may limit your job or career opportunities. Draw up a 2-column matrix, listing your strengths and skills. Focus on those things you do especially well and briefly explain how they might help you in a career or profession.

5. Write a memo to yourself, discussing your weaknesses and shortcomings. Focus on those things you can't do especially well, and explain *specifically* how you plan to go about dealing with those weaknesses. Describe the remedial steps you should take to acquire or improve your skills. Explain what you should do to cope with or to accommodate for those weaknesses or inabilities that you are unlikely ever to improve.

PERSONAL PROFILE AND CAREER PLANNING GUIDE

CAREER PLAN

Goal: _____

_____

_____

Targeted Positions:

After Graduation: _____

_____

Five Years After Graduation: _____

_____

ACADEMIC COURSES

Completed   Planned

_____   _____

_____   _____

_____   _____

_____   _____

_____   _____

_____   _____

_____   _____

_____   _____

_____   _____

_____   _____

_____   _____

Use a second sheet when filled.

ACTIVITY/WORK EXPERIENCE

Accomplished   Planned

_____   _____

_____   _____

_____   _____

_____   _____

_____   _____

_____   _____

_____   _____

_____   _____

_____   _____

_____   _____

_____   _____

_____   _____

_____   _____

PERSONAL INVENTORY

Profile:

Name _____

Year of Graduation _____

Home Phone _____

Home Address _____

_____

Local Address _____

_____

Local Phone _____

Self Description

_____

Skills/Strengths:

_____

_____

_____

CHAPTER 2

YOUR PERSONAL STATEMENT

Most people intuitively know that a Career Portfolio should contain such things as a copy of their resume, a cover letter to introduce them, a list of references, and perhaps a sample or two of their writing or professional abilities. For many, though, the idea of a "personal statement" seems a bit foreign.

"Is that the same as a career objective?" a student asked recently. "It's related to your career objectives," I replied, "but there's more involved."

"What do you mean by more?" he asked. "This is about more than what sort of job you want when you graduate," I said. "It's about who you are, what animates you, what you value, and who you hope to become." A personal statement is much more akin to the essay you wrote to accompany your undergraduate or graduate school application form. It's that first encounter a recruiter will have with you and may very well determine whether you get a telephone interview or a face-to-face encounter with a hiring manager.

That's a lot to ask of one small document. You're well-prepared to write it, though, and with some careful thought and a willingness to revise and think some more, you can get it done.

What It Looks Like

Most personal statements are not particularly long: rarely more than two or three pages with double-spacing between paragraphs and single-spacing within. That would give you a word-count of 500 to 750 words over several sheets of paper.

There is no format to follow. Professional career advisors say simply that you must seize your reader's attention and hold it to the end. This means that you should tell what is interesting and what will win your reader's sympathy and admiration. Vanity, self-serving praise, and ego-centric references are easy to spot and will rarely win friends or generate enthusiasm for you. Northwestern University's graduate school advises students to "make it clear that what you want is larger than yourself . . ." if you hope to influence decision makers.[i]

The statement should include your name and contact data at the top of page one. Unless your employer or graduate school application specifically asks for it, you should *not* include your social security account number. Insert page numbers at the bottom center of the second and third pages, but suppress the number on the first page. You'll find the commands to insert and suppress page numbers under "Format / Page" in most word processing programs.

Your Writing Style

Your writing should be fluent and reflective, not slick or glib. Avoid tired clichés, sensational language, and rhetorical flourishes. Keep your writing simple, fresh, and correct. Bad English and misspelled words are almost always noticed by those who matter the most and are frequently fatal to the essay. If people are looking for a reason to thin out that stack of applications on the desk, grammatical problems, spelling errors, and rough syntax are among the quickest of justifications for tossing your folder aside. Selection committees just don't give jobs, scholarships, prizes, or rewards to people they think are insufficiently literate or careless with words. That may seem unfair, but that's how it is.[ii]

How to Begin

As you begin your essay, you might brainstorm some of the following questions:

- What might help the evaluator better understand you? What sets you apart from other applicants? Who will be applying for the same job, program, or scholarships?

- Why are you interested in this field? What things have stimulated and reinforced your interest?

- How did you learn about this field (classes, seminars, work experience, the inspiration of friends or relatives)?

- Are there any unexplained gaps or discrepancies in your academic record? Are your grades and academic transcripts fully reflective of your intellectual abilities and work ethic?

- What skills or personal characteristics do you possess that would enhance your chances for success in this field?

- Why should a recruiter or selection committee be interested in you?[iii]

Writing the First Draft

Go back and have a look at your Personal Profile and Career Planning Guide, then review the answers you jotted down in response to the questions above. Gather as much useful information about yourself as you can and begin the first draft of your Personal Statement.

Try to find an angle or a hook that will catch your reader's attention. Give some thought to your opening paragraph and do your best to craft a couple of original, provocative, and thoughtful sentences. Hiring managers and selection committees will see any number of essays that begin with phrases such as, "Ever since I was little, I've always wanted to be . . . ," or "My lifelong ambition has always been . . . ." Worse, they will find no statement of ambition – only biographical details: "It was a dark and stormy night in 1986 . . . ." Skip all that. Save them the pain of reading things they can learn elsewhere, and share your professional ambitions and passions instead.

You might wish to begin with an anecdote or memorable incident that helped to define your life's direction or which helped you realize what you want to do in life. While such brief stories can add drama and vitality to a statement, be careful not make it melodramatic or cloying. You're hoping for an entry-level or advanced career opportunity that, presumably, does not involve writing daytime television scripts. It also helps, by the way, if the details of the anecdote are true. More than one job applicant has gotten into trouble by stretching or inventing details that he later had to recant and apologize for.

As you think about those issues or events that have provided you with professional direction or a clear career ambition, give some thought as well to the social value your aspirations. No one, absolutely no one, these days wants to hear about how much money you hope to make, what sort of house you want to own, how cool your wristwatch will be, or how fast your cars will go. A desire to "be the best" or to "achieve excellence" is one thing, but venal greed is another. If you're able to show how your personal and professional aspirations will contribute to the community, improve the lives of others, or make the world a better place (even just a little better), you'll win more friends and get a better reception every time.

Revise, Revise, Revise

Most folks aren't able to write a polished essay in one sitting. Such documents are usually the product of several revisions, each one eliminating small errors and improving on structure, word choice, content, and flow. If you begin with an outline of what you want to say – just the main points – and then develop sub-points for each of those, you may find it easier to write than if you simply begin with a blank screen and hope for inspiration.

Once the first draft is done, print it, read it carefully for content and flow, and mark it with a pencil. If you're particularly inspired at the moment, go ahead and revise what you've written and produce a second draft. For many writers, though, a little time and distance from an essay is helpful in refining both its structure and the details of expression. Come back to the project after you've had an opportunity to do something else and – this is important – *not* think about it for awhile. Your subconscious will give you some good ideas to work with when you return to the project a few hours or a few days later.

When you're ready to revise again, think about some of these issues:

- Does the opening paragraph grab your reader's attention? Is she motivated to continue reading or hoping this will end soon?

- Is your statement inherently interesting, or sleep-inducing?

- Is this a positive portrayal of who you are? Is it basically upbeat and confident? If you cannot demonstrate confidence in yourself, it seems unlikely that others will.

- Is it an honest portrayal? Would your family and friends agree that it's both accurate and fair?

- Have you answered the key questions: Why would anyone in this professional want to hire me? What makes me different, unique, or special? What are the most important strengths and qualities I bring to the workplace? What value will I deliver to the company that hires me?

- Does your Personal Statement provide any real insight into your character?

- Does it sound as if someone interesting, honest, and smart wrote it?

- Is it your best effort? Are the grammar, tone, syntax, spelling, and mechanics all correct? Have you eliminated 100% of the typographical errors?

For your final draft, be sure to avoid sloppiness, bad English, and unconventional spelling, as well as subject-verb and pronoun-antecedent agreement errors. Avoid whining, manufacturing a personality you don't really have, and displaying issues that reveal uncomplimentary or socially unacceptable biases and character weaknesses. Look for hints of arrogance or boasting, as well. Humility always plays well.[iv]

Time and patience are your allies here. Give yourself enough time to write this statement, think about it, revise it, and then revise it again. When you think it's done, show it to people who matter in your life: your parents, your professors, your advisors. Ask them to read it with a critical eye and suggest ways in which it might be improved. Eventually, after enough thought and revision, they'll tell you it's fine and ready for inclusion in your Career Portfolio.

What follows is a sample Personal Statement. This will be a bit different from the one you're planning to write. It was written, after all, by a student whose life, education, experience, and ambitions are different from your own. But it will give you some sense of what an authentic statement looks like and may reveal some of the thinking that went into its preparation.

Personal Statement of
Arianne R. Westby

Thomas Henry Huxley once wrote, "the rung of a ladder was never meant to rest upon, but only to hold a man's food long enough to enable him to put the other somewhat higher." Huxley poetically captures the timeless idea that life is less a destination than a journey. I believe our destination is important because it gives us something to strive for, but the true measure of success lies in each step of our journey.

I have carefully considered various career paths for my post-MBA work. Given my current work experience, and the knowledge I will acquire during my MBA education, I plan to pursue a career in Management Consulting. This career opportunity is a chance for me to gain exposure to a variety of industries, and to witness an array of corporate structures and management styles. It will also give me the experience I need to eventually launch my own consulting company, with an intended focus on helping small businesses and start-ups adjust to rapid growth and shifts in management structure. However, I aim to keep an open mind concerning opportunities I may not have previously considered. My experience has taught me that this can sometimes be the best avenue to success.

Knowing what skills I want to possess is as important as knowing the path I plan to pursue when I complete my MBA degree. My current skill set provides an excellent base for me to cultivate my entrepreneurial interests. I am eager to broaden my knowledge of various disciplines, since a solid business base is the foundation for sound management decisions. I am also hopeful to participate in the overseas study program in Chile. Exposure to different cultures and experience in international relations are assets in any industry. My current aptitudes will be refined at the Mendoza College of Business and translated into proficiencies that are valuable for a multitude of positions.

Over the past few years, I have developed skills in sales management, relationship development, pipeline maintenance, and e-business. I am one of just two Loan Officers in our company (a subsidiary of M&T Bank, with $29.8 billion in assets) who oversee the entire loan process, from application to closing, and all the details associated with the transaction. In most traditional cases, this would be split into three positions. Managing this variety of tasks on a multi-million dollar pipeline is a challenging responsibility. Due to my inter-disciplinary expertise, I am able to ensure smooth transactions for my clients and our mutual customers.

In order to successfully develop and implement strategic decisions, Management Consultants must understand how departments interact within a corporate structure. My experience of organizing a wide array of tasks has enabled me to see how the different aspects of this business are integrated, and how decisions made at one point in the process affect other areas. I also experience how employees are treated within an organizational structure, depending on their roles. Stereotypical assumptions about performance and aptitude occur regularly and can undermine the effectiveness of teamwork. By observing these issues, I have learned how to resolve conflict between different departments, and increase efficiency in production.

Relationship development in management is another area that demands focus and persistence. Few managers pay enough attention to these important skills. I am fortunate to have an excellent role model and mentor who taught me the value of cultivating solid relationships, both with clients and employees. Over the past few years, I have accumulated significant experience of my own. The relationships I have developed have become the foundation for my accomplishments as a Loan Officer. People are the greatest resource we have to achieve success. As a manager in any industry, you need people to trust your leadership. How you maintain relationships with your co-workers, vendors, and clients will determine your own level of achievement. These skills are pivotal to my intended goals in Management Consulting, since I will inevitably interact with many professionals in various environments.

I am a driven individual who pays attention to detail and enjoys working with people. I see learning as a continual process, and am eager to take the next step in my journey. I hope that it includes being a member of the incoming class of MBA students in the autumn of [this year].[v]

CHAPTER 3

YOUR RESUME

Many college students, and even some experienced professionals, think that a resume is just a summary of the jobs they have held, along with a brief description of the duties for each position. This is a popular misconception that can make it difficult for soon-to-be college graduates and those already in the workforce to know how to start writing their own resumes. Other popular misconceptions include a long-held belief that there is *one acceptable format* and *one acceptable method* to follow when writing a resume.

The truth is that there are numerous formats you can use, and just about any method that you have used for gathering information about yourself will work. Keep in mind that what you are doing is creating a marketing tool, a piece of print advertising, and the product you are marketing is yourself. This is not the time for you to be modest or self-deprecating; it is a time when blowing your own horn is most appropriate.

What is a Resume?

A resume is simply a document that gives potential employers an overview of who you are, where you've been, and where you hope to go. Its purpose is not to get you a job, as many people assume, but to get you an interview. Your goal is to entice a prospective employer into wanting to find out more about you in a personal interview, not to tell him or her everything about you in a couple of pages – an impossible task, even for the most experienced professional.

Another bit of useful information about resumes is that the average recruiter spends only thirty seconds scanning a resume. A sloppy or excessively wordy resume will be quickly recycled in the paper bin. This means that the content and layout of your resume should be concise and attractive. Learn to place your white space, bullet points, bold print, and underlines to take your readers' eyes to the information you especially want them to read.

Resume writing should be clear and articulate. Information should be easily accessible, and errors in spelling and grammar should be corrected long before the final copy is printed. Most career counselors suggest, and employers prefer, using a quality plain white or off-white bond paper. They also recommend that you limit the length of your resume to one or two pages at the most. College students and recent graduates should not plan for more than one page.

The Keys to Effective Resume Writing

The three C's – *clarity, conciseness,* and *correctness* – are the keys to writing an effective resume. Avoid the common mistake of starting each line of experience with "Responsibilities Included" or "Duties Entailed." This is also not the time to write complete sentences, despite what your English teachers always said about subjects and verbs. Instead, using an outline-type format for writing, start each sentence with a descriptive action verb that tells, as specifically as possible, what it was you did or accomplished in each position you plan to list.

What exactly constitutes work-related experience? Anything you have done that has prepared you to be effective in your chosen field, regardless of the title you held while you were doing it. This includes both paid and unpaid (volunteer) experience that clearly relates to your current career objectives. It would include summer jobs that may have no obvious connection to your career but indicate that you are reliable, punctual, hard-working, and have leadership potential. It also includes your on-campus involvement with organizations, clubs, activities and sports, along with special projects you may have completed as class assignments, such as senior seminar papers and honors projects.

A barrier that prevents many students from getting started on their resumes is not knowing what they're looking for in a first job and not knowing what skills, qualities, and characteristics employers are looking for in prospective job candidates.

If you don't know what you want in a job or haven't clarified your career goals, forget the resume for now. Instead, get to a resume workshop and schedule an appointment with your campus career planning and placement director. Remember, if you don't know where you're going, you probably won't get there. If you don't know what's important to you in your career and your life's work, you can't begin a job search. If you don't know what skills and personal qualities you have to offer an employer, you're unlikely to find a truly satisfying career.

Of course, that isn't necessarily all bad news, since many of us learn more from our mistakes than we do from our successes, and our first job often bears little resemblance to our later jobs anyway. It just means you're taking an unnecessarily circuitous route to the career satisfactions you really want.

What Are Employers Looking for?

On the other hand, if what's stopping you is not knowing what employers want, consider the findings of *The College Placement Council.* They surveyed college recruiters to find out what skills and personal qualities are most essential for new employees. Here is a list of sixteen attributes mentioned most frequently:

- **An ability to communicate effectively:** in speaking, writing, and listening.

- **Intelligence:** measured not by GPA, but an ability to generate ideas and solve problems.

- **Self-confidence:** measured by a willingness to take risks and undertake new experiences and projects.

- **Willingness to accept responsibility:** to accept a task and to take criticism when you make mistakes.

- **Initiative:** an ability to learn an operation and work with minimal supervision.

- **Leadership:** an ability to motivate and direct the activities of others.

- **High energy level:** a willingness to work hard and display enthusiasm, especially when the going gets tough.

- **Imagination:** the ability to solve problems and come up with innovative ideas.

- **Flexibility:** a receptiveness to new ideas and a real capacity for change, often on short notice.

- **Interpersonal skills:** the ability to get along well with others and bring out the best in them, even when they are very different from yourself.

- **Self-knowledge:** the ability to realistically assess your own capabilities and limitations.

- **An ability to handle conflict:** good stress management skills, as well as an ability to balance competition and cooperation.

- **Goal-orientation:** the ability to set and achieve meaningful goals.

- **Competitiveness:** as measured not only by athletic achievements, but also by academic and organizational success.

- **Vocational skills:** specific, technical skills required in your chosen field.

- **Direction:** a sense of career and goal-orientation.

Do these skills sound familiar? They should – most of them are the ones you've been developing throughout your education. There's no doubt about it – you have what employers want.

The next step is to look at what you've been doing for the last five-to-ten years that will prove you possess these important attributes. Take a note pad, some sharp pencils, a copy of your college transcript, and find a quiet place where you won't be disturbed. Use the top sheet of paper to identify the skills you possess that you would want a prospective employer to know about. These skills may be job-specific (technical skills), related to many professional areas of work (transferable skills), or qualities, characteristics, and working styles you have (personal management skills).

Use the next sheet of notepaper for each of these headings: education, work experience, volunteer work experience, and activities / organizations. Now, list under the appropriate headings everything you can think of that you've done that would indicate your abilities. At this point, it might be wise to include *all* of your experience; don't start eliminating possible entries for the resume until later.

Unless you did something genuinely spectacular in high school or preparatory school, such as serving as class valedictorian or student body president, you should limit your entries to your college education and extra-curricular activities. These note pages, along with your college transcript, will serve as worksheets as you develop your formal resume.

Writing a Resume that Works

Before you begin writing, you should have the answers to a few basic questions, including what resumes really are, how they're used by employers, and what they should contain.

What is a resume? As we mentioned a moment ago, a resume is a brief document – usually no more than one or two pages – that summarizes your ambitions and qualifications. It's a compact, quick reference that tells a prospective employer enough to know whether you're worth interviewing for a job.

How are resumes used? Employers frequently ask job applicants for a resume in order to determine the following:

- Level and extent of qualifications, including academic education, specialized training, and recent work experience.

- General suitability for employment in a particular industry, a particular organization, and – perhaps – a particular job.

- Specific functional area or division within a company that might be interested in this applicant. Many firms now use optical scanning devices to enter resumes into computers, then electronically search for the ideal candidate. Many large organizations, including the White House, The Walt Disney Company, and Ford

18

Motor Company, use software to analyze resumes, categorizing, for example, an applicant's primary work experience. Other businesses use less sophisticated technology that simply searches for key words. Career counselors have emphasized action verbs (*analyzed, wrote, directed, assisted*) in resumes, so that you can show what you've done. Now there is an equal emphasis on nouns that will catch the attention of an employer's software system (*Quark Express, financial analyst, bilingual*).[vi]

- Potential as well as performance. Most resumes are offered to an employer by people hoping to advance or move up. Past accomplishments are important, but only to the extent that they demonstrate future potential.

- Personal standards of neatness, organization, and self-expression in the job applicant. Your resume speaks volumes about how well you write, how closely you examine details, and how important you think neat, clean documents are.

What Should a Resume Contain?

Most resumes include four or five categories of information that would be useful to a prospective employer.

A heading. At the top of the page, you should include your full name, current mailing address, and a telephone number where people can reach you. If you have a fax number or an e-mail address, include those as well. Enter your name in capital letters and boldface type. Resume headings are usually centered or flush left, about an inch to an inch-and-a-half from the top of the page. If you are currently a full-time student living away from home, you should list your current address as well as a permanent address where employers can reach you during vacation periods.

An objective statement. Your resume should include a very brief statement about your near-term career objectives. This statement should say, in fairly specific terms, exactly what you are looking for, such as "An entry-level position in healthcare management." Or, "A summer internship in retail financial services." Your objective statement should mention keywords related to your background, education, qualifications, experience, and career interests. Above all else, please tell the employer what you want. Vague statements about "maximizing your potential" or "utilizing your creativity" won't do.

Your educational history. If you're still a college student, your education is probably your strongest qualification, so lead with that. In describing your educational background, briefly list the schools you have attended, starting with the most recent. Include the dates attended, degrees received, and major areas of study. Be sure to include the location of each school, as well. If you choose not to list your cumulative grade point average, be prepared to explain why you haven't. School-related extra-curriculars should probably be included under this heading, including activities, achievements, scholarships, honors, club offices, and athletics. Most resumes *do not* include high school or prep school entries.

Your employment history. Organize your work experience, beginning with your current or most recent employer. As you move backward in time, list the various jobs you've held. If you had more than one with the same employer, list the company name and location, then list position titles in turn. Talk in specific terms about what you did, rather than who you were. List responsibilities, scope of duties, and achievements; quantify wherever possible.

Additional information. This section would contain details of interest to an employer that don't fit easily into your educational or employment history. If you've worked as a volunteer, belonged to a civic organization, or had significant achievements outside of work or school, they should go here. Be brief but clear about what they are. Don't list personal qualities, describe your health, or talk about your ambitions in life. Simply provide information that might help a recruiter make an employment decision about you. Skill with specialized software, foreign languages in which you are (pick one: native, fluent, or conversant), or special certificates, licenses, or other qualifications might fit nicely under this heading.

Here are a few suggestions to consider as you begin writing.

- **Keep it brief.** Two pages tops; one page strongly preferred.

- **Include all relevant work information**, including companies and dates of employment. Omit street addresses and names of your supervisors.

- **Speak in terms of specific accomplishments.** Use concrete examples; quantify if possible. Use parallel form.

- **Use action verbs** to describe your skills and achievements:

analyzed	coordinated	improved
arranged	designed	maintained
assisted	distributed	organized
conducted	generated	trained

- **Keep it honest.** Don't puff up, cover up, or mislead regarding your accomplishments or compensation. Don't claim achievements that aren't yours. Don't list skills you do not have. If you weren't in charge, say "assisted . . ."

- **Target your resume for a particular job.** Use a text processing program to prepare different resumes for different jobs. Consider including the name of the specific company or organization to which you're applying in the objective block.

- **Study various models.** Experiment with arrangements. Use as few headings as possible. Consolidate. Keep in mind that while some arrangements work better than others, there is no one correct, universally accepted resume format.

- Consider including a **Summary of Qualifications** at the beginning.

- **Make it look good.** At the very least, your resume should feature quality paper, quality printing, judicious use of white space, standout headings, correct grammar, and correct, conventional spelling.

- **Write it yourself.** No one knows you as well as you do.

What to Avoid in Your Resume

In response to changes in our culture, technology, and employment, the fashion in resumes has changed. Today's busy human resource directors and hiring managers are looking for easy-to-read documents that reveal achievements and skills immediately. Some information is no longer considered useful or important.

Here is a list of information *you should not include*:

- **Photo.** Employers want to avoid any possible hint of discrimination.

- **Personal information.** Don't include hobbies, church affiliation, marital status, statements about your health, or other personal matters.

- **Salary Requirements.** Why price yourself out of a job or show that you're willing to work at bargain rates?

- **References** or a statement that "references are available on request." List them on a separate sheet and offer them at the interview.

- **Long paragraphs.** Use short statements or bulleted items.

- **Empty assurances.** All applicants, without exception, think they are honest, loyal, ambitious, and "people oriented." Demonstrate this through concrete examples on your resume and during an interview. "Books may recommend putting your hopes and dreams on your resume," writes *Fortune* magazine's Stanley Bing, "but let me tell you something as gently as possible: It's stupid. Nobody cares that you're looking for 'A personally expanding opportunity that will help me deliver on my potential as a developer of marketing concepts.' I'm cringing when I read it. Just tell me where you've worked and what you did."[vii]

- **Precise chronology of your life.** You do not have to account for every month of your life since you graduated from high school. Job applications may require this information, but not resumes.

- **Hobbies and outside interests.** Exception: Those that relate to professional interests or show traits and employer wants. You may want to think twice about listing any dangerous or time-consuming activities.

- **Date of resume preparation.** This indicates how long you have been looking for a job. Exceptions: when you are looking for seasonal work, such as a summer internship, or are about to graduate from college.

Remaining Honest and Truthful

One other, very important item to avoid in your resume is a lie. That would include falsehoods, untruths, half-truths, stretching the truth, puffery, misleading statements, or hints about things that just aren't so. A surprising number of job applicants are telling real whoppers on their resumes these days. *The Liars Index*, published by Wisconsin headhunter Jude M. Werra, is now at a record high. Werra checks the education claims on the 300 or so executive resumes he receives annually. In the first six months of this year, 23 percent of his applicants awarded themselves fictitious degrees, up from 17 percent the year before.

A number of high-profile executives have recently been caught stretching the truth about their credentials – among them, Ronald L. Zarrella, the chief executive of Bausch & Lomb, the eye-care products maker. Mr. Zarrella said he received an MBA from New York University, when, in fact, he left before graduating. The board of directors withheld a $1.1 million year-end bonus he had been promised.[viii]

RadioShack Corporation's president and CEO, David Edmondson, resigned in February of 2006 after the company learned that he had lied on his resume, claiming – among other things – that he earned two college degrees for which the school had no records. A preliminary investigation showed that he has attended a college in California for just two semesters and that the school didn't even offer a degree in psychology, which he claimed to have earned.[ix]

MCG Capital Corporation's chairman and chief executive, Bryan J. Mitchell admitted that he doesn't have an undergraduate degree from Syracuse University, contradicting at least 11 Securities and Exchange Commission filings by the company.[x] And Kenneth E. Lonchar left his position as chief financial officer at Veritas Software after the company learned that he falsely claimed to have an MBA from Stanford. His resignation followed on the heels of Sandra Baldwin, who resigned as president of the United States Olympic Committee after acknowledging that she had lied about her academic background.[xi]

It's not just executives who try to deceive employers with their resumes. Gary Hopkins, a spokesman for Tenet Healthcare, says his California hospital company checks the background of all applicants, from janitors to nurses. One out of eight, he says, has a hidden criminal record. Mr. Werra is puzzled by the resume inflation. Firms are so hungry for talent, he says, that "you don't need to lie." It's also risky because checking on what you say is easier than ever. For as little as $5, an employer can find out whether you really earned that MBA by logging on to sites such as www.edverify.com and www.degreechk.com.

"People are thinking, 'It's a competitive world out there, and I'm just going to get lost in the shuffle if I don't put my best foot forward,' even if it isn't true," said Robert P. Lawry, director of the Center for Professional Ethics at Case Western Reserve University in Cleveland. "But in the end," he adds, "you will get lost."[xii]

Padding a resume can take many creative forms: extending the length of employment so it doesn't look as though you've been out of work too long; changing a former job title, say, to account executive from executive assistant; or claiming to hold a degree when you're a few credits shy. Experts say some people have completely fabricated eye-catching positions at defunct and untraceable dot-com companies.

What should you do if you've stretched the truth or included an entry on your own resume that just isn't accurate? Most experts say the best approach is to come clean and admit what you've done. If you're still in school, that means revising your resume to make sure it's completely accurate and submitting a new version to your campus career center. That usually means that all previous versions will be deleted from their system and your revised edition will be posted. If you're employed, your choices aren't as easy. If the error is minor, you can simply submit an updated version of your resume without extensive explanation. Major misrepresentations that affect your qualifications for employment are another matter entirely. In such cases, you *will eventually be found out*, so it's best to admit the error early and ask forgiveness from your employer. Your boss will be much more likely to forgive a sincere, repentant employee than to retain an employee he has caught in a serious lie.

Non-Traditional Formats

What about offbeat, non-traditional, or wacky resumes? Won't an unusual approach get you noticed? Well, yes it may, but perhaps for the wrong reasons. When it comes to odd resume enclosures, employers and recruiters say they have seen it all: live animals (one candidate sent a puppy to a prospective employer), life-size mannequins, and even photos of candidates naked. Such efforts to stand out may increase as the economy cools down and the job market becomes more competitive. Many employers, however, say that far too often, job seekers aiming to look clever come off as creepy. While some suggest researching the company carefully before trying some eye-catching gimmick, most recommend simply playing it safe.

"The hiring party's aesthetic may not necessarily match yours," says David Opton, founder and chief executive of ExecuNet, a provider of job search and career management information in Norwalk, Connecticut. "Save your creativity for when you have more time with their attention."

The Creative Group, a Menlo Park, California firm that recruits marketing, advertising, and Web professionals, recently surveyed 200 advertising executives on the most unusual resume enclosures they had received, and posted responses on its Web site. Among them: a parakeet, a part of pants, and a steering wheel. The company advises job seekers to keep their applications professional and, when using gimmicks, to be careful. "You want your materials to represent who you are," says Lynn Taylor, a Creative Group vice president.

Classroom Projects

1. Identify six successful people in your city or community. Write a letter to each one, explaining that you are studying resume writing. Ask each of those people to share a copy of his or her resume with you. Together with a classmate, pool your collection of twelve resumes and look for the following: elements that they share in common, elements unique to one or more of them, layout, length, and arrangement of information categories. Prepare a brief presentation (five-to-eight minutes) for your classmates that summarizes your analysis of those resumes.

2. Using the twelve resumes you have gathered in project number one above, ask ten of your classmates to read each one briefly (no more than a minute per resume). Then, ask each of these ten people to *rank order* the resumes according to which ones they think are most effective. As your classmates sort through the resumes, make brief notes on which ones they like best and *why*. Keep track of which resumes they've read, awarding 12 points to the one at the top of the stack and 1 point to the last one. Add up the points your classmates gave to each resume and determine which resumes were most popular. You may either write up your findings as a paper for your professor or present them briefly (8-to-10 minutes) to the class.

3. Pay a visit to your local bookstore. Ask one of the booksellers to direct you to the *Business* section of the store. Examine at least six of the titles that offer advice about preparing resumes. On a notepad, write down the chapter headings for each book. Compare the headings of the six books you have selected, and analyze the similarities and differences. Note, in particular, those areas of advice which *all* of the authors provide. Note the areas that only one or two of the authors focus on. Finally, identify one book that you think is better than the others. Briefly (no more than three paragraphs) explain why you think that particular book is superior. You may either write up your findings as a paper for your professor or present them briefly (5-to-8 minutes) to the class.

4. Identify a local employer that requires resumes when hiring new employees. Arrange to conduct an interview, either in person or by telephone, with the employment manager. Ask that

manager several questions about resumes that he or she has seen in recent weeks. Which resume types are most impressive to him or her? Which resume types are least impressive? What sort of information does that manager want most from an applicant? What sort of information does that manager want least? Finally, has that employment manager noticed any trends lately (good or bad) in the resumes that he or she has received? You may either write up your findings as a paper for your professor or present them briefly (3-to-5 minutes) to the class.

CHAPTER 4

EMPLOYMENT CORRESPONDENCE

Among the least valuable and more dangerous bits of conventional wisdom among job seekers is the notion that cover letters are a mere formality, don't matter, or aren't ever read carefully. While it may be true that most recruiters don't spend a lot of time with cover letters, each of them will assure you that they look carefully at each of them for certain features.

What are they looking for? Most will tell you that the letter which accompanies your resume is the first bit of evidence about how well you communicate. It's also evidence of your level of professionalism, attention to detail, and sense of organization. Other recruiters say the cover letter can provide clues to your personality, and should begin to establish a relationship between the applicant and the organization. If you can't demonstrate in three paragraphs on one piece of paper that you deserve further, serious attention, your resume may never get read.

What Is a Cover Letter?

A cover letter, sometimes called a letter of application, is many things at once: an introduction, a personal sales pitch, and frequently a request for action on the part of the recipient. It gives the reader a sense of what's to come, not simply by summarizing the resume, but by showing how experience, talent, and interest will benefit the specific company it is addressed to.

Unless you are responding to an advertisement that specifically instructs you not to send a cover letter with your resume, you should always include one. They can serve many purposes. For example, such letters can:

- accompany your resume to inquire about possible job openings;

- respond (along with your resume) to a want ad;

- accept, reject, or show interest in a job following an interview;

- explain your career interests, job focus, or other issues that aren't immediately obvious in your resume.

Your cover letters should be:

- one-page, printed on a high-quality, laser printer;

- prepared on white or off-white bond paper;

- absolutely free of any typographic, spelling, or grammatical errors;

- addressed, if at all possible, to a particular person rather than a company, an office, or a division.

L. Michelle Tullier, whose book *Job Notes: Cover Letters* (Random House / Princeton Review Books) describes the art and process of drafting such documents, recommends that you sit down – just as we recommended in Chapter 1 – and think carefully about a number of issues before you begin that letter. Asking yourself these five questions may help you to better understand what that document should contain and how you should go about writing it:

- **What does this prospective employer need?** Which skills, knowledge and experience would be an asset in the job you are targeting?

- **What are your objectives?** Are you applying for a specific job, trying to get an interview, or simply hoping to get someone to spend 10 or 15 minutes on the phone with you discussing opportunities in general at that organization?

- **What are three-to-five qualities that you would bring to this employer or this job?** If you're responding to a job listing or classified ad in the newspaper, then those qualities should obviously be the job requirements mentioned in the ad. If you're not applying for a specific job opening, then think of which skills, knowledge, and experience would typically be valued.

- **How can you match your experience to the job?** What are at least two specific accomplishments you can mention that give credence to the qualities you identified in question number three?

- **Why do you want to work for this particular organization or person?** What do you know about the company? What is it about its products, services, philosophy, mission, organizational culture, goals, and needs that relates to your own background, values, and objectives?[xiii]

Writing a Cover Letter

Writing a cover letter isn't really difficult. Having gathered some information about the company, the job you want, and yourself, you're probably ready to begin. Structure your letter so that the information you want to convey fits neatly into three paragraphs: your introduction, the value you bring to them, and your request for an interview.

Paragraph one. In the first paragraph, introduce yourself and give the reason you are writing. You may be interested in the industry or in a specific kind of work. Perhaps you're responding to a want ad, or have been referred by someone who knew about a job opening. Gear your reasons for writing the letter to the interests of the person who will read it. The fact that you are unemployed or about to graduate from college and desperately need a job should *never* be included in a cover letter, resume, or interview.

Paragraph two. In the second paragraph, respond to the employer's question, "Why should I hire (or even interview) this person?" Describe in more detail any aspect of your resume that demonstrates:

- your interest or experience in this type of work, industry, or related area;

- your qualities as a worker; be specific, quantify where possible;

- how your education and experience will help you in this job or with this firm.

This is typically the most difficult paragraph of the three to write. It must be customized to every firm or organization you write to, and it must do more than simply repeat or summarize information that's plainly available in your resume. This is your opportunity to explain the value you bring to the company, to mention useful or interesting school and work experience, and to show your knowledge of the firm. Above all else, though, this paragraph must be brief – two or three sentences, cogently crafted. Get to the point, say what you mean, and move on.

Paragraph three. In the third and final paragraph, let the reader know if you intend to call for an interview, or if you will wait for them to contact you. "I look forward to hearing from you" is a positive approach. Be certain to include information about when, where, and how a prospective employer may contact you. That would include your e-mail address, a postal service address, and your home or dormitory telephone number.

One further tip: check the message on your answering machine. If it's a typically "cute" or smart-aleck undergraduate message, dump it. Put a professional response in its place. If your roommate recorded the message, have a talk about it.

Keep in mind that a cover letter isn't the place to summarize your background – your resume should do that. The cover letter is essentially a sales brochure, and it should be carefully crafted to stand out from the dozens, perhaps, hundreds of letters a company may get for a job opening. At the same time, it's also a "certificate of authenticity" and should contain only factual and accurate information.

"The best way to distinguish yourself is to highlight one or two of your accomplishments or abilities that show you are an above-average candidate for this position," writes Laura Morin in *Every Woman's Essential Job Hunting & Resume Book.* "You can also gain an extra edge by showing that you have some specific knowledge about the company and the industry," she writes. "This shows that you are genuinely interested in the job you are applying for – and that you are not blindly sending out hundreds of resumes."[xiv]

Larry Keller, a career writer with CNN.com, offers these suggestions, as well:

· Never address a letter to "Sir" or "Madam" or "To whom it may concern." Find out to whom it should be directed and address it to that specific person with his or her correct title and business address.

· Begin by explaining why you are writing, describe the skills and qualifications you have that are specifically related to the job you want, and close by restating your interest in the company.

· Use polite and professional language. Get to the point and keep the letter to just one page.

In their book, *201 Dynamite Job Search Letters*, Ron and Caryl Krannich write that many job applicants make a number of common mistakes in composing cover letters:[xv]

· Failing to communicate a clear purpose.

· Appearing unprofessional in form, structure and design.

· Spelling, grammatical and punctuation errors.

· Awkward language and use of the passive voice.

· Being overly assertive, boastful, and obnoxious.

· Appearing self-centered rather than job- or employer-centered.

· Saying little about your own interests, skills, and accomplishments or what you hope to achieve in the future.

· Addressing the wrong person or sending to the wrong place.

· Printing on cheap, unprofessional paper.

Here's one last test of a good cover letter. Pretend you're the corporate recruiter you've just written to. Open your own letter. You might be surprised how much a few minutes of role-playing would reveal about the approach you're taking.

Your List of References

Just about all job seekers know they will be asked for a list of references at some point in their career search. Selecting people to speak on your behalf is a particularly important part of the process and it's one you should give careful thought to before handing over a list of names to a corporate recruiter. Here are a few basic rules about references:

Select people who know you well. Don't ask friends of the family, casual acquaintances, or people whose job title you hope will impress a recruiter. Look for references who know about your academic performance or your work experience. If you're still in school, ask a professor who thinks you're smart if she would agree to serve as a reference for you. Very few of your professors will say "no." They do have a reputation to maintain, however, and will occasionally back away from a request that would put them in a compromising position. When asked by people whom they do not want to refer to an employer, most professors will say, "Why don't you ask someone who knows you a bit better?" If a student says, "You know me best," or "No one else will agree to do this," most professors will relent and agree to serve. Some, however, will be more direct and say, "I think you should ask someone who could write a good recommendation for you." Stay away from people who have absolutely no idea what sort of student or prospective employee you would make, including your dentist, your pastor, or business acquaintances of your parents. They may be important, but they just don't know much about your performance or potential as an employee.

Ask first. No surprises. Don't risk having one of your references say, "Really? I had no idea she was looking for work. I wonder what happened there." Worse, you could put someone in the position a colleague described recently when he received a telephone call from an employer in Chicago. "The manager on the other end of the phone said Susan Moss had listed me as a reference. Normally, I keep a folder of resumes near the phone for people I've agreed to refer. I looked in the folder and . . . no Susan Moss," he said. "I couldn't for the life of me even remember who she was." Embarrassing, to say the least, but worse for Susan. She didn't get a reference and, of course, she didn't get the job. Ask first, then send a thank-you note expressing your appreciation for the time and trouble involved in writing a letter or responding to a telephone interview.

Don't tell them what to say. It's both pointless and unprofessional to extract a commitment from anyone to say only nice things about you. What you really want them to do is help an employer make a well-informed, correct hiring decision. Many college professors and professional employers will warn an employer if the job description seems inappropriate for the applicant or if they see a bad skills-need match. The last thing you want is for you to get into a job that's clearly beyond your expertise or over your head and for your career to get off on the wrong foot. The purpose of reference checking is really two-fold: first, is this person who he says he is, and does he have the credentials and experience he says he does? Second, is the vacancy in the prospective employer's company appropriate for this particular candidate? Just ask your references to give an honest appraisal of your performance and your potential.

Update the contact data. Make absolutely certain you have accurate and up-to-date contact information for each reference, including cell phone numbers and e-mail addresses. A complete reference entry would typically include: first and last name, and middle initial; job title; corporate or organizational name; postal service mailing address and zip code; office telephone number; mobile or cell phone; and preferred e-mail address. Interviewers can gather additional information once they've made contact. Do not include home telephone numbers or personal e-mail addresses unless you've been asked or given permission to do so.

Keep the reference list separate. Do not routinely attach your list of references to your resume. Print a number of copies and keep them in a folder separate from other documents, but ready to hand to an interviewer who asks for them. We mentioned in Chapter 3 that you should not include an entry on your resume that "References are available upon request." Of course they are. If they're not available, you won't be hired.

Follow-Up and Thank-You Letters

The interview is not the end of your job search. You absolutely must maintain contact with each potential employer, demonstrating that you are grateful for their time, that you enjoyed meeting and speaking with them, and that you are actively interested in employment with their firm.

During the concluding minutes of an interview, establish a time line that you can follow. Make sure you leave the interview with the recruiter's name, title, and phone number. Ask for his or her business card. Also, learn when you can expect to hear from him or her, and when he or she expects to hear back from you.

Send a thank-you letter the same day, if you can, but certainly within three days of the interview. Include the following information in the letter:

Paragraph one. Thank the interviewer for the interview. Mention the date and location of the interview, and include the title of the position you are applying for.

Paragraph two. Restate your interest in the position and the company. Mention anything that you think was especially important from your conversation with the recruiter. Show a willingness to provide any additional information and/or clarification of your skills and background.

Paragraph three. Say that you look forward to hearing from him or her and conclude with a positive statement.

Based on the time line developed, follow up with the recruiter. For example, he or she may have said that you would hear from the company in a week; if you haven't received a call or letter, respond with a letter (not a call) of your own. Don't be overeager, but do stay in contact.

Write first, then follow up with a phone call. Be polite but persistent.

Keep looking. Don't stop your search because an interview with one company went well. Continue to network, send letters and resumes, and look for opportunities to interview. Your goal is to have several job offers and then to select the one that suits you best.

You'll find samples of various forms of employment correspondence, including cover letters; follow-up, thank you-letters; and acceptance letters in Appendices A and B.

CHAPTER 5

RESEARCHING THE COMPANIES YOU MOST WANT TO WORK FOR

Finding the right job involves more than just deciding what you're good at, or what you'd be happiest doing each day. It also involves finding out as much as you can about the firms and organizations you're considering. Just as they want to find out all about you, so you should want to find out all about them.

Why should you research the firms you plan to apply to or interview with? There are two reasons, really. First, the more you know about a company or an organization, the easier your decision will be. Second, employers expect you to research them, and they'll be looking for evidence that you've done your homework.

Employers expect you to research them for a number of reasons. Your investigation helps a prospective employer to determine your level of interest and enthusiasm. Careful research will demonstrate your understanding of an effective employment interview. Finally, if you thoroughly research a company *before* you interview with them, it leaves a favorable impression on that employer.

Beginning Your Research

Here are half-a-dozen tips for researching companies you think you might like to work for:

1. Publicly-owned companies are usually easier to find information about than privately-held firms. Finding detailed information on Ford Motor Company, for example, will be substantially easier than finding information on Cargill, the agricultural consortium, because Ford is publicly held. All public companies are required to file documents with the U.S. Securities and Exchange Commission (www.sec.gov) and numerous sources are available to help you learn more about such companies. *Business Week* (www.businessweek.com) magazine publishes an annual directory of the world's top 1,000 corporations; *Fortune* (www.fortune.com) publishes a similar guide to the nation's 500 biggest companies.

2. Corporations as a whole are generally easier to find information about than their subsidiaries or divisions. While you'll find information easy to come by on Ford Motor Company, you may find that gathering information about the Ford Light Truck Division is not as easy. The company's web site (www.ford.com) will provide you with information the company wants you to know. The company's Corporate Communication Division or Investor Relations Office would be another good place to begin. Time permitting, you may even consider writing to or calling the company to ask if they could provide information for you. Many companies,

unfortunately, will simply refer you to their Web site, but it may be worth your time to talk with them anyway.

3. Large, nationally-known or global corporations are always easier to find information about than local or regional firms. Again, Ford is a company that's known world-wide for its motor vehicles. Arvin Meritor, on the other hand, is not as well known. Arvin Meritor is a tier one supplier to the automotive industries and Ford happens to be one of their best customers. Arvin Meritor is a public company, though, so if you're persistent, you'll find what you need in some of the directories listed below.

4. Information found in a library may be somewhat dated, perhaps as much as several months or years old. If you're interested in historical data about a company, a bound volume in your local library might be a good place to start.

5. Current periodicals, journals, and electronic databases are more likely to have fresh information. The *Dow Jones News Retrieval Service*, for example, will list everything that's been printed in recent years in *The Wall Street Journal* (www.wsj.com). If you've heard that Arvin Meritor is planning to expand, has acquired another firm, or is planning to produce a new line of automotive products (useful information to know if you hope to interview with them), *The Wall Street Journal* story about their plan would be available online.

6. No single library will have everything you need. You should consider visiting public libraries as well as your school or college library, chambers of commerce, government offices, trade associations, and other sources. Information is expensive to maintain and libraries often specialize in certain kinds of information, so you will have to look carefully as you conduct your research.

Preparing for Your Interview with Useful Information

If you're hoping for a job interview with a particular company, the *minimal research* necessary would include the name, industry, and size of the organization; its reputation within the industry; the firm's principal products or services; and its office or plant locations.

A more thorough job of research would separate you from other job seekers and would probably include the name, pronunciation, and title of your interviewer; the regional or branch office locations of the company; its industry position, market share and profitability; the company's annual earnings; its recent growth, including mergers and acquisitions; the company's organizational structure; any training expected or required by the firm or the industry; and, of course, the company's principal competitors.

Bill Goodwin, Manager of Human Resources at Bayer Corporation's North American Headquarters in Pittsburgh, Pennsylvania, says, "If you don't know anything about us, you can't get an interview. It's as simple as that. We would expect you to know about our business, our products, and something about our industry. Beyond that, it's up to you." What sorts of things would impress him? "I'm not impressed if you know yesterday's closing stock price of Bayer Common," he said. "But I would be very impressed, for example, if you knew that we just invested $170 million in an advanced polymers processing plant in Baytown, Texas." Why would he be impressed? "Two reasons," he replied. "First, it tells me the applicant is paying attention to the company and to the business. Second, it's flattering to have someone confirm what you already believe about your company. We think it's a great place to work, and when others come in here and tell us *why* it would be a great place for them to work, we're impressed."[xvi]

Research Sources. It would be nice to know all that – and, perhaps, more – but where do you find such information? A number of readily-available sources will help. You might begin with reference books, such as the *Directory of Corporate Affiliations, the I & S Index of Corporations and Industries, Dun's Million Dollar Directory*, or *The Thomas Register of American Manufacturers*. To find financial information, you might try *Standard and Poor's Register, Moody's Industrial Manual, Moody's Bank and Finance Manual, Moody's Municipal and Government Manual*, or *Moody's Transportation Manual*. Other comprehensive references include the *Value Line Investment Survey*, and *Standard and Poor's Analysts Handbook*.

If you're looking for current information in print about business or investment activity involving a company you've targeted, try *Advertising Age, Business Week, CPA Journal, Dun's Review, The Economist*, the *Federal Register, Financial World, Forbes, Fortune, Harvard Business Review, Nation's Business, The New York Times, Newsweek, Personnel Management, Time, U.S. News & World Report*, or *USA Today*. Unquestionably, the most valuable day-to-day tool for understanding business people and the way business is done in the North American market and around the world is *The Wall Street Journal*. Reading it once won't give you much insight, but reading it each market day will provide you with a comprehensive understanding of commerce, industry, finance, and business issues in this country and abroad.

You should also consider other sources of information about the industries, professions, and companies you're interested in, including corporate annual reports; corporate magazines, newspapers, and newsletters; product brochures; corporate news releases and public announcements; stock research reports; and online databases. You might also consider speaking with current or former employees of the companies you're most interested in.

What about prospective applicants for entry-level positions with companies such as Bayer Corporation? "If a job applicant has been reading *The Wall Street Journal, Business Week*, and other general business publications, he or she will know a great deal about us. But," added Goodwin, "when an applicant cites information she's read in *Chemical and Engineering News*, we know she's serious." Goodwin confirms what Human Resources managers and college recruiters have told students for years: the more research you do on a firm you want to work for, the easier your interview will be, the better the impression you'll leave with the recruiter, and the more informed your decision will be. Research is work, but it pays off in more offers for second interviews and better long-term employment opportunities.

Finding Business Information on the Internet

The Internet has become a remarkably useful tool, both for business people and for students studying to become one of them. Hundreds of millions of computers, linked together worldwide, have instantaneous (well, perhaps immediate) access to information by, from, and about businesses across the globe.

The Internet, however, is not without its problems. For one thing, the information it contains is not organized. Stephen Hayes, a university business services librarian, has described the Internet as "a library with all the books on the floor." It's no ordinary library, either. Literally anyone can set up a home page, buy an address, and begin doing business on the Internet. The United States Supreme Court ruled in 1997 that government censorship of Internet content is unconstitutional. So, a student in search of information can – and often does – find inaccurate information alongside something of value on the Internet. "There's little we can do to verify the accuracy of the information contained in most sites on the World Wide Web," said Mr. Hayes. "Thus, each of us should approach what we find with appropriate caution and skepticism – just as we would a print source."

The World Wide Web is organized broadly into four categories of sites: government, educational, commercial, and not-for-profit. Internet addresses, known as URLs, reflect this in the letters they contain. Corporate home pages (usually ending in ".com") will tell you things about a company that they want you to know, such as where to buy their products, how their stock price is doing, and how to apply for employment the company. In many ways, it's simply another form of advertising.

Government-sponsored Web sites (ending in ".gov") provide large categories of information, including census data, international trade and banking data, and regulatory information. These sites usually have a legal mandate to maintain the authority of the data. Educational institutions, such as colleges and universities, sponsor Web sites (ending in ".edu") that permit students, alumni, and others to find out more about everything from academic curricula to how the varsity lacrosse team is doing.

Finally, Web sites sponsored by not-for-profit organizations (usually ending in ".org"), such as the American Red Cross, Goodwill Industries, and National Public Radio, offer everything from program schedule and broadcast transcripts to detailed descriptions of current activities in their organizations

Search engines and directories are among the most useful tools to someone looking for information on the Internet. Simply speaking, search engines and directories are programs which will search for information that you ask about. If you visit www.yahoo.com, you will find one of the most popular and widely-used directories. Simply type in the keywords that best describe the product, service, company, or industry that you want information about and the Yahoo! directory will produce numerous references with links to Web sites that may prove useful. *Directories* will search only the higher levels of a Web site, such as the title and author, while *search engines* will explore deeply into the data requested.

The more precisely or narrowly you define what you're looking for, the greater the chance that one of the more widely-used search engines will find what you're seeking. Among the more popular search engines are www.HotBot.com, www.AltaVista.com, www.NorthernLight.com, www.SearchEngines.com, www.JetEye.com, and www.Kaboodle.com. Most of you know, of course, about a *very* innovative and enormously popular software package at www.Google.com.

Web sites with information about business are numerous and easy-to-find. Here are some addresses that may prove useful as you look for information about business on the Internet.

Alta Vista (www.altavista.digital.com) A powerful search engine and index tool used to locate information about products and companies. Includes a full-text index of Usenet news group archives, offered by Digital Equipment Corporation.

Babson College Business Resources (www.gopher://info.babson.edu:70/11/.bus/) Sources and sites for information about business, international resources, entrepreneurship, market reports and government.

Business.com (www.business.com) An interview almost always ends with that question you don't know what to do with: "Any questions for us?" A search here turns up press releases. You can show you've done your homework by referencing their latest marketing campaign or asking them about the new Corporate Ethics Officer.

CareerPath.com (www.careerpath.com) Newspaper employment ads from major U.S. cities. A good place to find out how the competition plans to expand. A free service but it requires registration.

CEO Express (www.ceoexpress.com) This innovative, one-stop portal provides you with an Internet search engine, a Web directory, stock search engine, and more. Among the most interesting features is a direct, one-click link to hundreds of free, current business publications online, including domestic and foreign newspapers, magazines, wire services, health sites, broadcast operations, weather services, and package-tracking sites. If you enjoy reading business information online and want access to breaking news around the world, this is an excellent place to start.

Deja News (www.dejanews.com) Search for discussion groups by keyword, personal name or discussion group name.

Excite (www.excite.com) Leads to a number of useful, selected Web sites.

Stat USA, United States Department of Commerce (www.stat-usa.gov/stat-usa) A great source for *all* statistical data gathered, processed, and published by the United States Department of Commerce. Caution: This site requires a $50 annual subscriber fee.

FedStats (www.fedstats.gov) This new site from the U.S. government effectively layers a powerful search engine on top of statistics-laden sites for a variety of government agencies. This approach far surpasses navigating the maze of individual federal Web sites. Agencies include the Bureau of Labor Statistics, the National Center for Education Statistics, the Bureau of Justice Statistics, the U.S. Bureau of the Census, among others.

Federal Web Locator (www.law.vill.edu/Fed-Agency) Government information compiled by the Villanova Center for Information Law and Policy. Extensive listings categorized by government branch.

Competitive Intelligence Guide (www.fuld.com) Fuld & Co.'s competitive intelligence site. Offers analytical tools, links to other intelligence sites.

Hoover's Online (www.hoovers.com) Company directory listings searchable by company name, location, industry and sales figures. Thousands of company capsules outline financial data, list key competitors, and link to related news articles. If a potential employer talks up an IPO and dangles stock options, get the offer price and other facts at the IPO Central section.

Infoseek (www.infoseek.com) Includes Usenet news groups and non-Internet databases. Offers additional databases, including wire services, for a fee.

Lead Story (www.leadstory.com) The day's top news story, bristling with informative links from AT&T.

Library of Congress Catalog (www.loc.gov) The ultimate library catalog. Can help locate obscure books.

Lycos (www.lycos.com) A top search tool. Includes summaries of pages.

Nation Job (www.nationjob.com) This database for job seekers allows you to search by salary level. Type in medical jobs in the Northeast paying at least $50,000, and a long list pops up, including pharmacists, dentists, and drug sales reps.

The NETworth Equities Center (www.networth.galt.com) The Investor Relations Resource on this site is a searchable index of Web pages published by public companies.

NewsLink (www.newslink.org) More than 3,000 links to news-oriented sites.

New York Public Library (www.nypl.org) This is clearly the finest public library on-line; virtually limitless resources.

Patent Portal (www.law.vill.edu/~rgruner/patport.html) Site for patents and patent law.

The Riley Guide (www.rileyguide.com) For more information on researching companies, and other job-search tips, visit career consultant Margaret Riley Dikel's site.

Salary.com (www.salary.com) This Web site can help answer the question, "Am I being underpaid," or "Are they offering me enough money?" This is the broadest salary-comparison site on the Web. Its Salary Wizard allows you to pick a job category and a region and to quickly find median salaries by position. A manufacturer's rep in Detroit can expect a base salary from $43,926 to $64,380, for example. There's also news on compensation and benefit trends, and "Ask Annette," an online advice column.

Society of Competitive Intelligence Professionals (www.scip.org) Home page features publications, electronic discussion groups, expert/speaker database, and events calendar.

Starting Point (www.stpt.com) Home page links to major U.S. companies.

U.S. Census Bureau (www.census.gov) This is a fee-based electronic subscription service that provides convenient access to popular Census Bureau databases. CenStats also provides direct links to databases with common geography (i.e., counties, ZIP code areas, and census tracts).

U.S. Department of Labor (www.dol.gov) At this site, you can determine which jobs have the greatest potential for growth, along with median annual salaries for each. One downside: salary data are less fresh than at other sites.

U.S. Securities and Exchange Commission (www.sec.gov) Offers 10-K and reports filed by public companies, as well as lots of interesting investor education documents.

Vault.com (www.vault.com) This site will give you the inside scoop on employment perks at thousands of companies, covering everything from the "chichi code" at Conde Nast to on-campus services available at Silicon Valley's Oracle. Interviews with insiders ensure that the 3,000-plus profiles reflect a company's culture, including hallway gossip.

Virtual Library (www.loc.gov) This web site, managed by the Library of Congress, lets you look up information on almost any subject imaginable. Some virtual browsing may spark your creative instincts.

The Wall Street Journal (www.wsj.com) Dow-Jones, Inc. publishes an on-line version of the *Journal* each business day, complete with feature stories, closing quotes, and other interesting business-related information. This site requires registration and an entry-code, but for now there is no charge to use the service.

The Washington Post (www.washingtonpost.com) A great on-line version of the nation's most politically-focused newspaper. All the net basics in plain English.

Yahoo! (www.yahoo.com) Among the most popular directories; will lead you to numerous web sites.

Finally, perhaps the best site on the Web for information about business and the new economy is operated by the publishers of *Fast Company* at www.fastcompany.com. Their newly revised site is divided into Career Zones with timely, personalized content designed to help guide you through the difficult issues facing job seekers, entrepreneurs, managers, and executives. Each microsite's home page is updated twice a week with Web-only stories and magazine articles that provide action items, resources, and solutions tailored to your interests. In each of the ten microsites, you can find a job, freelance, find fast companies, research salaries, rate a company, join a discussion, solve a problem, network, ask the experts, or receive a tutorial on life in the new economy. Here's a real plus: every one of *Fast Company*'s issues and articles is now available online for free, graphics and cool colors included.

In the last analysis, you should understand that the Internet is a source of some very good, very useful information, but it's certainly no substitute for good library resources and skills. For more information on the Internet or other sources of information about business, see a professional librarian.

Selecting an Ethical Employer

The most important decision you can make in making your next career move is to select an employer whose values match your own. It's clear that no employer will change its value system just to accommodate you, and changing your own closely held values to accommodate them will be painful, if not impossible. The best advice is simple: select an employer whose values are parallel to yours. You'll feel better about what you do, who you represent, and how you earn a living each day.

The current wave of corporate scandals is pushing more job seekers to greater lengths to gauge prospective employers' ethical standards and practices. They are poring over Internet message boards looking for staff members' appraisals of management, checking financial histories, and seeking meetings with present and former employees. The risk: it's all but impossible to uncover everything about a corporation's moral weak spots in advance.

Many students say they are afraid of joining an unethical employer whose behavior could jeopardize their tenure, career prospects, retirement savings, and self-esteem. As countless Arthur Andersen, Enron, and WorldCom employees have discovered, working for a business with a damaged reputation can also impede future job prospects by leaving a black mark on a resume.[xvii]

Many companies have begun to notice heightened concerns about ethical standards among both job seekers and recent hires. Patrick Gnazzo, Vice President of Business Practices for United Technologies Corporation in Hartford, Connecticut, says the reason a number of job applicants "came to UTC is that they had researched our ethics program." His company began a program nearly 20 years ago that lets employees inquire anonymously about ethical issues. The program has logged nearly 56,000 inquiries.[xviii]

Some businesses resist prospects' inquiries about their less-than-comprehensive ethics programs, though. You should view such hesitation as another reason to look elsewhere. "If an organization is uncomfortable with you asking questions, then I would say that's a sign right there," says Professor Linda K. Trevino of Pennsylvania State University's Smeal College of Business. She recommends an "ethical culture audit" for students and others seeking employment. Among the questions she thinks you might want to ask a prospective employer are these:

- Is there a formal code of ethics? How widely is it distributed? Is it reinforced in other formal ways, such as though decision-making systems?

- Are workers at all levels trained in ethical decision making? Are they also encouraged to take responsibility for their behavior or to question authority when asked to do something they consider wrong?

- Do employees have formal channels available to make their concerns known confidentially? Is there a formal committee high in the organization that considers ethical issues?

- Is misconduct disciplined swiftly and justly within the organization? Is integrity emphasized to new employees?

- How are senior managers perceived by subordinates in terms of their integrity? How do such leaders model ethics-related behavior?[xix]

In the final analysis, it's your career that's at stake here and your personal reputation that you must safeguard. The most important question to ask yourself may very well be: "Is this an organization I would be proud to work for, or is this just another source of income?" Alternatively, "Will people think more of me, or less of me, if I reveal the name of my employer to them?" When you have your next batch of business cards printed, your name and that of your employer will be on the same 3.5"-by-2" card for all to see. When you hand your card to a colleague or acquaintance, you don't say, "Here's my employer's card." You say, "Here's *my* card." You're also saying, "This is who I work for. This is who I am." Are the business practices, values, and ethics of that company the same as your own? Are you genuinely pleased to say that you are a member of this organization? If so, you've chosen the right company. And they might say, in return, that they're pleased to have chosen the right employee.

CHAPTER 6

MARKETING YOURSELF ONLINE

Don't let the banner ads fool you. Finding a job on the Internet isn't just a few mouse clicks away, but using the Web sure beats the traditional methods of job hunting.

The speed and scope of the technology revolution have surprised business professionals everywhere. Even so, the revolution is spreading at breakneck speed over the world of job hunting and hiring. In recent years, the online network has turned into a bustling job bazaar where you can market your talents, find out what openings are available, and maybe even land the position of your dreams.

Whether you have just met the corporate axe or are entering the job market for the first time, the online possibilities are too big to ignore. Of course, the time-honored method of sending out printed resumes still works. But given the changes taking place, it would be a smart move to supplement your envelope licking with some online inquiries.

Within just a few minutes of logging on, you could find several hundred help-wanted postings in your field, call up in-depth analyses of companies that interest you (in references such as SEC 10-K filings or *Hoover's Handbook* of company profiles), schedule meetings with professional job counselors, and get sample resumes to help you write your own.

You can find job openings on the Internet, or on the easier-to-use part of it called the World Wide Web, or on the commercial online services such as *America Online, CompuServe, Prodigy,* or *MSN*. Among the best sources of job ads, resumes, and career-related information on the Internet is the *Online Career Center* (www.occ.com). It was started in1996 by six companies – Aetna, Alcoa, IBM, Eli Lilly, Monsanto, and Procter & Gamble – and now has nearly 300 corporate members, each of which pays an annual fee to join and list available jobs. Job hunters can browse and put up their own resumes free.

In another venture, six of America's biggest newspapers, including *The New York Times* and *The Los Angeles Times*, are now offering their combined help-wanted advertising online at www.careerbuilder.com. Pam Dixon, co-author of *Be Your Own Headhunter Online* (Random House), says "The perception is that if you're on the Internet, your IQ automatically goes up ten points." For that reason, she adds, some high-level, high-tech jobs are advertised only online.

James C. Gonyea, author of *The On-Line Job Search Companion* and creator of America Online's Career Center, produces *Help Wanted – USA*. It puts more than 10,000 job ads weekly, as varied as accountant and zoologist, on *America Online* and the Internet. Delphi, an online service that is now a part of a *NewsCorp/MCI* joint venture, has a specialty in the entertainment business; job seekers can speak online with TV and film producers.

Pam Dixon recommends that you prepare not just one resume but two, and post them on employment databases as well as e-mail them to individual companies on the Net. The first resume should be the standard one-page text version, with heavy emphasis on keywords (such as, "computer," "finance," or "profit") that would leap out in a recruiter's sweep of the Net. The second should be a more detailed description of your accomplishments with appropriate graphics, perhaps even some audio comments in your own voice. Your goal, she says, is to snare a talent scout with the first resume, and sell him or her with the second.

Getting Hired by Getting Wired

The best-known general-career sites include www.Monster.com, www.HotJobs.com, and www.CareerBuilder.com. Monster.com is clearly the biggest of these in terms of the number of job postings, with more than 800,000 active postings from companies and recruiters by January 2006. ComScore Media Metrix, an Internet audience measurement company that counts Web traffic, says Monster was the #10 Website (and #1 among job sites) on the Internet during 2005. Visitors logged on and spent an average of 22 minutes at the site surveying ads, posting resumes, and learning about salary ranges.[xx]

Web traffic to career services sites jumped 26 percent in 2005 to some 50 million visitors. Traffic at CareerBuilder climbed 74 percent last year with more than 21.2 million visitors a month. Monster saw a 38 percent increase to 14.5 million visitors, while Yahoo! HotJobs rose 19 percent to 8.5 million visitors. Career counselors like the HotJobs site for its easy-to-use format. It also doesn't have any ads from headhunters and employment agencies, and many job seekers who prefer to deal directly with employers seem to like that.[xxi]

Job.com hosts more than 2 million visitors per month and features about 13,000 active postings at any particular moment, with a total of more than 650,000 per year. Employers seem to like the job.com website because of pricing policy, while job seekers appreciate the relatively low candidate-to-employer ratio.[xxii]

GetHired.com is a somewhat more specialized, New York company that teaches job-finding skills. David Schmeir's firm shows job-seekers how to identify companies that are hiring and how to distinguish yourself from the rest of the crowd through effective self-marketing. His services are not free, though they are more comprehensive and personalized than those of the general-career sites. Tele-workshops via phone lines and the Web can help spruce up your interview skills and sharpen your focus for a fee ranging from $1 to $150.

Whatever site you choose, searching and targeting jobs on the Internet is quick, relatively simple and safe, as long as you don't do it on a computer owned by your current employer. If you are currently employed, you should know that your employer monitors the e-mail and web site traffic on company-owned computers and may very well begin reading about what you've been up to. To be blunt about this: looking for work on your current employer's computer and e-mail system is *not* a smart idea.

To use one of the large posting services, simply type in a keyword, skill, location, job title or company names, and out comes a list of potential jobs. If a listing looks promising, you can send a resume. Job seekers can typically use a site's services free of charge. For each position advertised, employers will pay anywhere from $95 for a 30-day listing to $275 for a 60-day listing. They also receive volume discounts.

Niche-marketing web sites. Robin Baker, a 31-year-old art therapist, missed being around children when she worked at a Philadelphia geriatric out-patient facility. She liked earning her living helping people, but she wanted to work with kids. So, she started looking for a new job.

She tried newspaper classified ads first, but found no match there for her joint degree in art therapy and special education. When she logged onto the Internet, it was a different story. She spotted some possibilities on the web site of a trade group, the American Art Therapy Association (www.arttherapy.org), but on a regional site (www.phillyjobs.com) with 3,500 jobs in metropolitan Philadelphia advertised, she hit the jackpot. She typed in the keywords "teacher," "mental health," and "art therapy." Up came her dream job: an opening for a special education coordinator-art therapist at a charter school in nearby Chester, Pennsylvania.

Niche sites like the ones Ms. Baker visited are cropping up all over the Internet, harboring a wealth of information from professional groups, trade associations, geographic regions, and companies ranging from corporate giants to Internet start-ups. The advice, according to *The Wall Street Journal*'s Beth Mantz, is to begin with portal sites, such as www.rileyguide.com or to use one of the search engines listed above.

The basic rules for a successful job hunt haven't been changed by your ability to search online, says Gary Resnikoff, president of CareerMag.com, whose Web site has about 100,000 job listings. He suggests that job seekers craft their resumes with industry terminology and references that will cause employers to slow down and look carefully, or uncover the resume if they run a "find" search through the Internet. Job seekers should also exhibit caution. Just because an employer has a Web site or job postings on the Monster board doesn't mean you necessarily want to work there, or even want to talk with them. The same concerns about a personal values and a good cultural fit are just as true on the Internet as they are in your college career center or the "Help Wanted" section of your local newspaper.

Making the most of your computer. College career counselors offer these six suggestions for making the most of your computer during a career search:

- List your computer skills on your resume, even if you are not looking for a high-tech job.

- Do not include your Internet home page address on your resume unless you have groomed the site for a business audience.

- Include your e-mail address, and check for messages frequently.

- Don't expect companies to open your e-mail attachments. Always send another copy of your resume and cover letter as (cut-and-paste) text e-mail messages, by fax, or by postal service.

- Before going to an interview, visit the employer's web site. Know what's on it.

- For the most part, getting your foot in the door still means getting your foot in the door. Videoconference interviews and online or telephone interviews may be a useful first step, but your aim is to line up in-person interviews when you can.

What to Avoid in Online Job Hunting

Joellen Perry of *U.S. News & World Report* says job-search sites are everywhere these days, and so are mistakes on the part of eager online job hunters. Old fashioned virtues, including careful proofreading, politeness, and persistence still pay off. Here are a few common mistakes to avoid:

- *Format faux pas.* Web resume data banks don't take Word documents, so posting online requires reformatting to the plain-text American Standard Code for Information Interchange (ASCII) with no frills like bolding or underlining. Rule of thumb: use only symbols on the keyboard, such as an asterisk instead of a bullet point. Avoid e-mail attachments wherever possible, because many of them may not convert. Instead, cut and paste your resume into an e-mail message.

- *Limited postings.* On warehouse sites like www.monster.com, employers pay a fee to list jobs and scan resumes. "You'd be wise to also post someplace like www.careers.yahoo.com or www.flipdog.com, where recruiters graze for free," says Susan Britton Whitcomb, author of *Resume Magic*. Also seek sites aimed at your field: try a search engine and words such as "jobs" and "consulting."

- *Failure to follow up.* For about a dollar a pop, a blasting service like www.resume.machine.com or www.resumeblaster.com can shoot your resume to HR departments and provide a list of employers who received it. You should phone to see if it arrived intact and to answer any questions they may have.

Hold the ads. True Web resumes – personal web pages showcasing your skills – are mostly awful. A common gaffe is using free Web-hosting services such as GeoCities or Lycos, which flash ads alongside your resume. "That's about the tackiest thing I've ever seen," says Pat Kendall, president of the National Resume Writers Association. Also avoid going overboard. Just because you have access to 87 different colors doesn't mean you have to use all of them.

Classroom Projects

1. Work together with two of your classmates to assess career-search services on the Internet. Identify between 8 and 12 online job-search and resume-posting services you each can visit. Make a brief list of features, strengths, and (if you can spot them) weaknesses of each service. Include information about cost and the number of available job offerings on each site. Share your information with your classmates in a brief presentation that focuses on what they can obtain online inexpensively and (perhaps) for free.

2. Contact your campus Career and Placement Center and obtain their advice regarding online job search and resume posting. Find out whether they will permit you to post your resume on the college or university's server and inquire about such issues as format, specific categories of information, and whether they will accept MS or Corel text files, or if your resume must be in ASCII or HTML format. Share that information with your classmates in a brief presentation that focuses on what steps they must take to post their resumes online with your school.

CHAPTER 7

INTERVIEWING FOR A JOB

Digital age technology has made it easy to gather information about employers and the publicly-traded firms they work for. The Internet, corporate annual reports, and promotional literature are ready gateways to information about prospective employers. In addition, a wide range of online services and electronic data bases makes it easy to find prospective employers.

Finding those with employment opportunities, open positions, and a career path that is well suited to your education, talents, and ambitions is another matter. The temptation to print hundreds of letters and stuff them into hundreds of envelopes, along with a generic copy of your resume, is all too real. The numbers alone tell a chilling tale: 200 blind mailings will yield, on average, just one promising job interview.

A targeted job search, on the other hand, involves careful research of the industry (or industries) you want to work in, the firms you'd most like to work for, and the entry-level jobs open to people with your qualifications. That takes time, thought, and focus. The payoff is worthwhile, though: 200 targeted contacts will yield, on average, 20-to-25 promising job interviews. Careful research is the key to a successful job search. And, once you've found the firms you'd most like to work for, successful interviews don't happen by accident. They require thorough and careful preparation.

In a full-scale job search, finding a few initial interviews isn't all that difficult. Many college placement services, in fact, will provide you with an opportunity to sign up for interviews with recruiters visiting campus. Many companies conduct informative, informal briefings about their products, services, people, and career opportunities. Typically, representatives of such firms will accept a resume during those sessions and, if possible, arrange to meet with you to discuss employment opportunities.

Goals of an Interview

Once you've managed to land an interview, keep in mind that you have four basic goals to accomplish: to provide information to an employer about yourself; to gather information about that employer and the job that's offered; to make a decision about whether to accept a job, if one is offered; and finally, to find a situation that's a good match – a good cultural fit between you and the company, and a good fit of skills and needs.

During a first interview, however, you have a more immediate series of objectives: first, you must get the interviewer to like you. If this doesn't happen, of course, a second interview (and subsequent job offer) is out of the question. Finally, you must convince the interviewer that you should be invited to the company for a second interview.

Planning for an Interview

Successful interviews don't happen by accident. They're the result of a great deal of careful planning, hard work, and preparation. If you've chosen to interview with a company for the right reasons, if you've done your homework and are ready to sell yourself and your skills to a recruiter or employer, your chances for an invitation to a follow-up interview are good.

Many college students know precisely what they want to do for a living. Many, in fact, have career plans mapped out well in advance of graduation and have a carefully-culled list of companies they plan to approach for employment. Others, including some who are very near graduation, haven't any firm notion of what they will do, or how they will begin a career. If you're one of these latter types, or are just flexible enough to consider many different possibilities, you should begin formulating interview strategies as a part of your job search.

The first of your pre-interview strategies is to carefully examine the companies you've researched and select only those in which you are likely to be a "good cultural fit," that is, compatible with the views, beliefs, habits, and ways of life in those firms. Second, make sure you seek an interview for the right reasons. "I need a job" may sound like a good reason to you, but it won't impress an interviewer. You ought to have at least one really good reason why you'd like to work for them or they won't hire you. Finally, you should prepare a series of questions you want answers to – questions that are directly related to the job or employment category being offered. The more you know, the better off you'll be. The better prepared you are, the more likely it is you will get a second interview.

What are Interviewers Looking For?

"We're looking for someone with intelligence, coupled with interpersonal skills," says Jeffrey M. Christopher, Sales and Marketing Manager with R. J. Reynolds and Company. "Did they listen to the questions I asked? Did they understand them? Can they interact intelligently with me for thirty minutes? Did they not only answer the question, but provide some level of detail?" "At Reynolds," he adds, "we're looking for influencers. Can this person command the attention of someone who doesn't report directly to them?"[xxiii]

Brent Switzer, Human Resources Manager at Oscar Mayer, looks for those things and more: "We look for maturity, practical intelligence, social skills, and evidence of innovation." Is grade point average important? "Sure," he says, "but it's only one measure. I want to know if you have leadership skills, an action-orientation, an appetite for responsibility. Look, there are so many good people out there, you've got to do your absolute best to convince me that you're worth a second look. Your energy and enthusiasm level during the interview are important."[xxiv]

Larry Langford, Corporate Staffing Manager at Taco Bell Headquarters, looks for both traits and behaviors during an interview. "I want to know if you're a leader, but I also want to know how you responded to specific job demands and responsibilities. I also look for integrity in a job applicant. High energy levels and interpersonal skills are important, as is eagerness to build relationships. But I'm also looking for people who know how to do the right things. If they show me they can do that, they'll get a second interview."[xxv]

"I'm looking for a good cultural fit," says Stephen Achilles of Cap Gemini Ernst & Young Consulting. "I go after the practices, behaviors, and habits you display, and ask whether or not you'll fit in here. If you respond to certain management requirements or job-related situations in the way we would expect, you may be the sort of person we're looking for. If you won't be happy in our culture, or can't respond to the demands of our customers, then you won't succeed here. It's just as important," he adds, "that you know who we are as it is for us to know who you are."[xxvi]

Is appearance important? "It's the first thing we see," Achilles says, "and I think it's very important." Baxter International's Kay Wigton offers an old cliche in interviewing: "You only get one chance to make a first impression," she says. "Make it a good one."[xxvii] "Appearance is important," according to Chicago banking executive Lynn Lillibridge, "but I'm not turned off by splashy neckties or an upscale business dress. At least that shows some personality." Unshined shoes, a rumpled suit, or a dirty, frayed skirt just won't do. "The most important part of a man's appearance is his shirt," she added. "It should be clean, fresh, and crisply pressed."[xxviii] Sarah Hamil-Bajac of Deloitte & Touche, LLP says, "The quality of clothing is less important than how carefully it's been cared for."[xxix]

What Turns Interviewers Off?

We've talked about the odds before – your chances of getting a second interview are about one in fifty. And the chances of your getting a job are about one in a hundred. Frequently, the reason many people aren't hired – even though they're technically qualified and perfectly good workers – is that the interview didn't go well. And, when asked about it, recruiters are unusually candid about what turns them off.

"People who hedge their answers," says Hamil-Bajac, *especially* when specific replies or facts are available."[xxx] "Anybody who's not truthful," says Jeff Christopher of R. J. Reynolds. "Don't embellish your accomplishments, add to or stretch the truth. If you increased sales by five percent, don't say it was fifteen."[xxxi] "Someone who's looking for a job based solely on money," observes Brent Switzer of Oscar Mayer. "If your principal interest is money," he says, "either don't tell me, or look for work somewhere else. We want people who are interested in contributing to the organization. If money is the main driving force, we're not interested."[xxxii]

"Improper grammar is a show-stopper for me," says Larry Langford of Taco Bell. "People who use double negatives or who clip their words probably aren't going to represent our firm well. I'm also offended by untruthfulness or serious inconsistencies in people's stories."[xxxiii]

Mark Peterson of Procter & Gamble agrees: "It turns me off to meet people who can't get their stories straight," he says. "Don't make up details as you go along. When I ask you for a number, be accurate or tell me you don't know. I'll find out if you've fabricated something or lied to me. In sales," he observed, "you manage people from a distance, and if you can't trust them, you've got to get rid of them. It's better never to have hired them to begin with."[xxxiv]

Here are some other issues that can sabotage an interview and prevent you from ever getting a second chance with a company.

Personal appearance. People who are improperly dressed or simply not prepared for the occasion send precisely the wrong message to the interviewer. If you're going to represent that firm, they're going to expect you to live up to their standards. That's true, even though you are not yet an employee. You may be living and working in one world (school), but you're being held to the standards of another (business). Business communication consultant Carmine Gallo says, "If you want to be taken seriously, inspire confidence, and establish a presence, start by dressing for success."[xxxv]

Attitude problems. People who are indifferent, upset, angry, hostile, or insouciant will turn off an interviewer in a hurry. You've got to do your best to be pleasant, cooperative, forthcoming, and likeable during an interview. After all, the recruiter is considering whether or not you should be a co-worker and a member of his or her company.

Poor self-expression. Bad grammar, improper English, poor sentence or paragraph structure, profanity, racist or sexist language, or extreme hesitancy in expressing yourself may keep you from being invited back.

Lack of interest. Surprisingly, some people just don't appear to be interested in the job, the company, the industry, or in the interview itself. Your mood is transparent and readily interpreted by the interviewer. Show some enthusiasm, display a positive, upbeat attitude if you're really interested in the job.

Resume gaps. Holes in your resume which go unexplained will cause the interviewer to suspect you're trying to hide something. If you list a couple of years in college, followed by an unexplained gap and then a return to college, you'll want to talk about why you left school, how you spent your time, and your reasons for returning. Be honest, don't hedge your response or say what you think the recruiter wants to hear. He or she will find out what the truth is, despite your best efforts to disguise or embellish it.

Lack of social skills. Basic social graces, including appropriate verbal and nonverbal mannerisms are important to most recruiters. You'll represent their firm, you'll carry the company logo, and people will think of the firm when they think of you. Therefore, corporate recruiters want people who can handle themselves with grace and dignity, and who'll feel at ease with many different kinds of people. Inappropriate nonverbal mannerisms are the first tip that you may not be the sort of person that company is looking for.

Weak handshake. This may sound trivial, and to many people it is, but not to a corporate recruiter. Your handshake is the first form of contact a recruiter will have with you; make it a strong, confident and positive experience.

Lack of eye contact. In the North American business culture, an unwillingness to make frequent and sustained, direct eye contact is perceived as a lack of confidence and trust. Interviewers and business contacts will invest much lower levels of both in a person who won't look them in the eye. It's not the same in other parts of the world, but on this continent and in much of Europe, looking people directly in the eyes is a positive sign.

Evasive Answers. People who hedge their answers, couch their responses in vague or nebulous terms, or people who fabricate replies are asking for trouble. "If I catch a candidate lying to me," says one *Fortune 500* recruiter, "the interview is over right then and there." Honesty is not only the best policy, it's the only policy. You're not required to reveal everything, and some issues are clearly beyond the bounds of what's reasonable for an interviewer to ask about. But if you choose to reply, you are obligated to do so truthfully.

Absence of Tact. Akin to social graces and business communication skills, tact is the ability to speak and act without offending others. It's the ability to say and do what is appropriate to the audience, the situation, and the occasion.

Excessive Interest in Salary or Fringe Benefits. You should never speak about money during a first interview. And you should speak about it in a second interview only when the recruiter brings up the subject. If you display a keen interest in compensation, vacation schedules, health insurance, retirement programs, and other issues peripheral to the job, very few employers will be interested in you. Keep your focus where is should be: on the job.

Lack of confidence. Recruiters will often note a lack of self-assurance, poise, or confidence in a candidate and quickly brand him or her as a poor prospect for employment. It's okay to be quiet or reserved. It's even acceptable to be shy. But you've got to project your very best sense of self-assurance when you meet with an interviewer, demonstrating that you're at ease with different types of people and ready to handle whatever comes your way.

Inadequate match. More than anything else, an inadequate match between the company's needs and the applicant's skills and background will sink an interview. Usually, applicants don't make it to the interview stage if they're unqualified for the job being offered, but sometimes they'll seek out an interview anyway. If you're not hired right away, it may well be a mismatch between job requirements and your skills, qualifications, and experience that prevents it from happening. Read the offerings and go after those for which you are best qualified.

Mock Interviews

Consider conducting a practice interview, or perhaps two, before you meet a recruiter for the real thing. Rehearsing your interview skills in a "mock interview" with a corporate representative, faculty member, classmate, or close friend may well improve your odds for success during a real job interview.

What is a mock interview? It's a 30-to-40 minute videotaped session of you in an interview with a professional. Just about all colleges and universities will provide you with an opportunity to rehearse your interview skills with a Career and Placement Center professional or, perhaps, an alumnus from a company that recruits on your campus.

How should I prepare? Prepare for a mock interview just as you would a session with a real recruiter. Gather information about the industry, the company, and the position you're hoping to land. Look for the most commonly sought traits in that business, such as analytic skills, communication abilities, business knowledge, teamwork, or leadership. Write out the answers to the most difficult questions you are likely to encounter, then rehearse your replies. Work through each of the questions and answers until you are thoroughly comfortable with your replies. Self-confidence is a huge issue among college recruiters and you'll be much more confident if you've had an opportunity to practice.

What happens during a mock interview? The same sort of things occur in a mock interview as would happen in a real interview, except for the assessment. You should dress appropriately, greet the interviewer with a firm handshake and an enthusiastic smile. As you begin, let the interviewer take the lead and respond to her questions, just as you would if this were the real thing. Listen carefully to what she says and make sure you know what the interviewer is looking for. If you need clarification on a question, ask for it, but be cooperative. Your responses should be brief and concise: no more than two or so for each. Even with factual questions ("Are you a senior now?") or seemingly directionless questions ("I see you're majoring in Marketing. How's that going?"), you should do your best to respond to the reasons for which they were asked. Be friendly, forthcoming, and cooperative as you try to get a conversation going. And, even though this is a mock interview, have at least a few questions prepared to ask the interviewer.

The assessment. When the interview is done, your interviewer will give you an opportunity to watch the videotape and observe yourself as a prelude to a more complete feedback session. Watch carefully as you respond on tape to the interviewer's questions. Observe your non-verbal mannerisms and mood. Are you confident? Do you convey enthusiasm for the company and the opportunity you're seeking? Have you come across in the way you intended? When the interviewer begins providing feedback, listen with an open mind. Do your best not to be defensive; she's just given half-an-hour of her time to help make you better at this. Learn from your performance by seeing yourself as others see you.

Telephone Interviews

Many employers, in order to save money and decrease the probability of inviting the wrong candidate for a face-to-face interview, will often resort to preliminary interviews by telephone. These can be stressful events, but you should look at them as an opportunity to begin a dialogue with people who have a professional vacancy that you'd like very much to fill.

The principal advantage to a telephone interview, from your point-of-view, is that you can prepare notes and keep them in front of you as you talk. You also don't need that freshly pressed shirt and interview suit for a phone conversation. The disadvantage is that you can't make eye contact with your interviewer and many of the other non-verbal cues we all rely on during personal conversations are simply missing. Keep in mind that the recruiter on the other end of the phone is facing the same dilemma and must take all of her cues from your vocal mannerisms. Be enthusiastic, professional, and courteous.

Job hunters often mistakenly believe that phone interviews are less formal than face-to-face meetings. Most recruiters will tell you they're a critical first hurdle in landing a job. Mindy Gikas, a managing director in the New York office of Ogilvy Public Relations Worldwide, was interviewing a manager on the phone last October when suddenly the job candidate paused. He said he was reading an e-mail. "It showed me that his conversation with me wasn't very important," she said. He wasn't invited to interview in person.[xxxvi]

Interviewers hear everything during telephone conversations from flushing toilets to clamoring dishes and barking dogs. "If you have scheduled a conversation," says Chris Wilkins, a strategic staffing manager at Ingersoll Rand Company, "plan to be in a quiet place." If the call was unexpected, it's perfectly alright to ask if you can reschedule.[xxxvii]

Given a phone interview's lack of eye contact and body language, candidates are evaluated largely by what they say and how they say it, according to recruiters. Interviews listen for clues indicating such qualities as passion for the job, professionalism, and whether the person might be a good cultural fit. In May 2005, Ruth Bielobcky, principal of Ion Design LLC in Frederick, Maryland, rejected a candidate for a senior copywriting job because she wasn't able to get a sense of who he was. "I couldn't imagine putting him in front of a client to communicate a concept, because you need to have enthusiasm and intonation in your voice to sell."[xxxviii]

A couple of suggestions as you prepare for a phone interview: research the company carefully, keep your notes and resume in front of you, and don't forget to mail a thank-you note to the interviewer that recaps your best selling points. An e-mail thank-you is insufficient.

Case Interviews

Management consulting firms began offering case interviews to their prospective employees during the early 1990s, and many other businesses have been quick to join in. You'll find these sessions widely used to screen candidates for consulting, financial services, public accounting, marketing, and executive positions. Case interviews test your ability to solve problems and think big without having real data in front of you. Questions such as "Why are manholes round?" or "How many gallons of water are in Chicago area swimming pools?" are just warm-ups. "Ford Motor Company is thinking of modifying its best-selling light truck models. What issues should the company think about before making any changes?"

Analytic thinking is the product of your education, your work and social experience, and more. You can't simply become a logical thinker overnight if you haven't had any preparation for that. You could ask one of the business professors on campus for a case study that you could use to prepare yourself for such an interview, or you could contact Bain and Company, a San Francisco consulting firm, for insight. Their advice for applicants:

> We value the case interview process *as a means for us to get to know each other* better. It is a chance for you to show us how you think through *a real business problem* and for us to work through an example of the kinds of work we see everyday. For this reason, our interviewers prepare their *interviews based on real cases* and tend not to rely on brainteasers or theoretical problems.

> What are they typically like? A good case interview should be an enjoyable and *thoughtful discussion of business issues* and problem-solving techniques. We are not looking for a "right answer" or asking you to spit back memorized business terms, current events or well-known frameworks. Rather, *we hope to see a good dose of problem-solving skills*, creativity, and common sense. A good interview will be fun and full of energy!

> How do you "ace the case?" Your answer should reflect *structured thinking* in which you: break the problem down; focus by prioritizing which areas to investigate; demonstrate clear analytic evidence based on assumptions, math and logic; and make an actual recommendation. At Bain, we look for *recommendations* that are actions designed to *generate results*, not merely academic answers.[xxxix]

If you're confronted with a case interview, don't panic. You've been asked to analyze and solve a number of problems before, so this one should be no different. Remember to show your assumptions, the logic path you employ, and the outcomes you envision. And, above all else, your interviewer will expect to see an action-oriented set of recommendations. That, beyond all else, is what managers do: take action to solve business problems. And that's precisely what they're looking for in your thinking.

Behavioral-Based Interviews

An increasingly popular approach to interviewing focuses less on what an applicant thinks or feels about his or her skills and achievements, and hones in on very specific incidents in that applicant's job history. Sometimes referred to as *critical incident interviewing*, the technique is also known as *behavioral-based interviewing,* and tries to elicit responses that will help an employer find out more about specific, job-related behaviors. Those behaviors will, presumably, tell an employer a great deal about how you are likely to behave in the future if those situations arise in the job you're applying for.

Paul Green, a leader in the behavioral interviewing field, sees an interview as a part of a process, rather than a single event. That process, he says, begins with an analysis of the skills needed to perform a particular job, followed by a definition of those skills in very specific terms. Once that's complete, employers then develop questions based on the skills they've identified, and only then will they call a job applicant in for an interview.

In this form of interviewing, employers will ask open-ended questions – that is, they will ask questions which are worded in a way that encourages a candidate to open up and be talkative. They will also take notes during the course of the interview, tolerate silence from a candidate, seek contrary evidence to balance the picture the interviewer receives, and control the interview to prevent a candidate from wandering off track or being elusive.

Employers using critical incident or behavioral-based interviewing will probe a candidate's responses in ways that are directly related to the job skills they've already defined. Often, questions will be phrased to a candidate by using the exact wording contained in the skill definition. This not only helps to focus the interview, it can also help the employer avoid potential legal entanglements in the interview.

Questions that emerge from this interview technique are used to help reveal such things as good organizational and time management skills: "Describe for me a day you had planned when you were approached with an emergency of higher priority. How did you handle this? What was the outcome?" Other inquiries might include questions used to evaluate:

> **Your ability to communicate directly and openly:** "Give me an example of something complicated that you had to explain to others. What were the results?"

- **Conflict resolution skills and stress management:** "Give me an example of a recent time when you had a performance issue with a subordinate – for example, absenteeism, chronic lateness, or not following company policy. How did you handle this?"

- **Honesty and integrity:** "Have you ever discovered a fellow employee doing something which you knew to be wrong? How did you deal with it and what were the results?"

- **Accountability for actions:** "Tell me about a time when you had a deadline to meet and other people did not perform their work properly. What did you do? How did it turn out?

- **Good decision-making skills:** "Describe for me a recent decision you made. What were the circumstances? How did you reach your decision? What was the outcome?

- **Your ability to serve as a positive role model:** "Has there ever been a company policy or procedure you felt was inappropriate? How did you handle this? What was the response of your superior?"

- **Your ability to support others:** "What do you do when someone makes a mistake and you discover it? Give me some examples. What were the results?"

- **Your ability to live with ambiguity and work in grey areas:** "Can you tell me about a time when something came up on your job and there was no official procedure for handling it? What did you do? What happened?"

- **Your ability to give positive feedback and recognition:** "Tell me about a time when you observed that your subordinate put forth an extra effort. What did you do?"

- **Teamwork skills and team spirit:** "What did you do the last time someone other than your supervisor asked you to do something that was not part of your routine job description? How did you feel about it?"

- **Your ability to know and do what is expected:** "Tell me about the most recent mistake you made on your job and how you handled it.

These are just a few of the dozens of questions an employer might ask in order to elicit responses that focus on specific skills and abilities you have. Those are skills, remember, that are directly related to the job you're applying for. An interviewer using questions of this sort won't let you duck one of them just because you don't have a good answer ready. An interviewer will usually just wait and let you think of an incident that fits the question he or she has just asked.

If you look puzzled or confused, an interviewer may rephrase the questions, but you won't get off the hook simply by saying, "I can't think of anything just now." The reply is likely to be, "Take a minute to think some more. An answer will come to you." That sort of technique can really put you on the spot if you're unprepared. To succeed in a behavioral-based interview, you must provide answers that demonstrate that you understand the question and why it's being asked.

In such interviews, you cannot fabricate an answer – that just won't do. If you haven't had a job-related experience that would help you answer the question, respond by describing a similar situation that may have arisen while you were on an athletic team, in a fraternity or sorority, or participating in an extra-curricular activity at school. A lack of job experience shouldn't prevent you from answering questions that are designed to see what sort of skills and abilities you have. Chances are, you have plenty of skill. You must be prepared to illustrate how those skills have been used in actual job or school-related situations.

Getting Ready for the Real Thing

Monster.com, the world's largest online career-search firm, encourages you to prepare a checklist to help get ready for an employment interview. Here are some of the ideas they suggest:

- Purchase professional-looking correspondence paper (stationery and matching envelopes).

- Keep enough paper on hand to print your resumes, cover letters and other correspondence on matching stationery and envelopes.

- Know the standards for writing cover letters and thank-you notes, and when to use the phone.

- Keep enough first-class stamps on hand to correspond with employers.

- Keep track of all career-related written correspondence and telephone conversations in separate folders, organized by company.

- Identify your basic interview wardrobe: select one or two outfits or suits that are considered fairly conservative for your field.

- Locate your local overnight or one-hour dry cleaner. Keep at least two clean, freshly pressed shirts on hand and polish your business shoes.

- Always have extra, clean copies of your resume with you.

- Keep an interview folio or folder to bring with you on interviews. It should contain a few extra copies of your resume in a plastic sleeve, some reminders for yourself about your skills and goals, along with a reliable pen and some paper to make notes before, during, and after the interview.

- As you depart for the interview, make sure you have your folio, the names of the people your are meeting, and directions to the interview room. You may also want to bring a comb, some Kleenex or a handkerchief, and a few breath mints.

- Give yourself plenty of time. You want to arrive early, not just on time, and never late. Bring a newspaper or business magazine to read while you're in the waiting area.

- Follow up with a thank-you letter immediately (same day). Check your e-mail, voice messages, and postal service mail regularly. Make sure people know how to get in touch with you, and be diligent about replying.[xl]

Once you've done your research, tried a mock interview, reviewed your checklist, and buffed the shoes, you should be ready to meet a professional corporate recruiter.

CHAPTER 8

THE DAY OF AN INTERVIEW

Once you've signed up for or secured an interview, make sure you're ready. Be certain you know where and when the interview will be held, how you will get there, what you will wear, who the interviewer will be, and what sort of job you will be interviewing for. Review the questions and checklists in this book, just to assure you've done everything possible to prepare.

Interview Objectives

Remember that your interviewer's objective is to hire someone to fill a vacant position. Your ultimate objective, of course, is to find a rewarding and satisfying job. First, though, you must focus on near-term objectives:

· Get the interviewer to like you;

· Get the interviewer to listen to you;

· Portray a confident, positive, enthusiastic image;

· Get the interviewer to invite you back for a second interview.

Very few firms ever make an offer of employment to college graduates during a first interview. The objective of a first interview, from their viewpoint, is to screen out undesirable candidates. Real employment decisions are made after a second interview, often conducted on company property, rather than on campus. Some large firms may require three or more interviews before they're ready to make an offer.

What to Wear

The answer to this question is easier than you might imagine. Wear your best business suit. Dress as you would for a mid-morning business meeting in which you might make a presentation. Your attire should be conservative, sensible, and upscale, but not flashy.

For men, a grey or blue business suit of a weight suitable to the season. A white shirt, clean and well pressed, complemented by a solid, striped, or conservatively patterned necktie in silk or poly-silk blend. Dark, patterned, or textured dress shirts are in vogue among many business professionals, but you might save those for on-the-job wear once you've been hired. As conservative as it may seem, the freshly-starched, white dress shirt is always a good choice.

Dark, over-the-calf socks and a plain, dark belt should complement your shoe style and color. Shoes may be anything from a blucher to wing-tip or cap-toe style, but they should be leather dress shoes, well shined with new laces. If you've lost or gained a significant amount of weight recently, buy a new belt. That tell-tale crease in your belt won't send the right signal to an interviewer.

For women, a conservative two-piece business suit in grey or blue is the best choice. A conservatively cut skirt in wool or poly-wool blend, complemented by a jacket on matching or contrasting colors is customary. A white or matching-color blouse with tie, neckscarf or accessory pin at the collar establishes a professional look for a woman seeking a professional position. A one-piece shirtwaist dress or stylish skirt and blouse will do, particularly in warmer climates, but the absence of a jacket puts your wardrobe at the low end of the acceptable attire scale. Remember, professional or managerial women wear suits; secretaries and administrative assistants wear dresses. Matching shoes in mid-height heels and neutral beige or taupe stockings are customary, as well.

What *Not* to Wear

For men, the answers to this question are easy, as well. Don't wear something you would wear to a casual or informal function. That would include shorts, jeans, golf shirts, patterned trousers, checkered or plaid pants, shirts, and jackets. Footwear should be professional and business-like in appearance. That would exclude running shoes, sneakers, sandals, boots, and woodsy hiking gear. Jewelry should be confined to a wristwatch and ring and, perhaps, small or unobtrusive cuff links. Chains and earrings are unacceptable for men.

Women are similarly constrained in what not to wear, though they do have a few more options than men. Spike heels in excess of 2-1/2 inches; open-toed shoes; short, tight skirts; sheer or transparent blouses; patterned stockings; and excessive jewelry are off limits. Accessories and make-up should be low-key and conservative in nature. Hairstyles may vary widely, but should generally reflect a clean, well-kept appearance, neatly brushed and combed. Hair bands, bows, pins, and clasps are fine, as long as they complement the rest of your appearance and don't specifically call attention to themselves. Needless to say, shorts and pants won't do, and neither will sports or casual attire of any sort.

The safest rule to follow is one passed along to a young associate by an advertising agency vice president some years ago: "If you want to be one of us," he said, "you'll have to look like one of us." Do you want to work in banking? You should try your best to look like a banker. The same applies to the professionals who work in whatever business, industry, or profession you'd like to join. Pay careful attention to how they dress and conduct themselves;

take the time and effort to pattern your appearance and manners after those you most admire. You won't be far off the mark.

The National Association of Colleges and Employers recently conducted a survey of hundreds of employers for their publication *Job Outlook*. Among the questions they asked of employers was the extent to which the physical appearance of job candidates might influence their hiring decisions. "Personal grooming" was rated as having the greatest influence on an employer's opinion, followed by "nontraditional interview attire," and "handshake." Such issues as "nontraditional hair color," "obvious tattoos," and "body piercing" were close behind. Having very little effect on their views of a job seeker were such issues as "beards" and "mustaches."

You may wish to consult a book on professional presence. Among the best are *Five Steps to Professional Presence* by Susan Bixler and Lisa S. Dugan (Adams Media, 2000), and *Buff and Polish: A Practical Guide to Enhance Your Professional Image and Communication Style* by Kathryn J. Volin (Pentagon Books, 1999). You might also consider *The New Professional Image: Dress Your Best for Every Business Situation* by Susan Bixler and Nancy Nix-Rice (Adams Media, 2005). John T. Molloy's *Dress for Success* (Warner Books) is a classic. These and similar books will give you some sense of what to wear, how to care for your wardrobe, and how to look your best in the workplace, no matter what the dress code.

What to Bring with You

At a minimum, you should bring your letter of appointment or invitation, directions to the interview location, and a clean copy of your resume. You should also being along a small, professional-looking notebook and pen to take notes or write down any specific instructions your interviewer gives you. Taking notes on a PDA or Palm Pilot is probably just showy (and probably slow) at this point. If you use a hand-held computing device to store appointments, however, be sure you update your files after the interview.

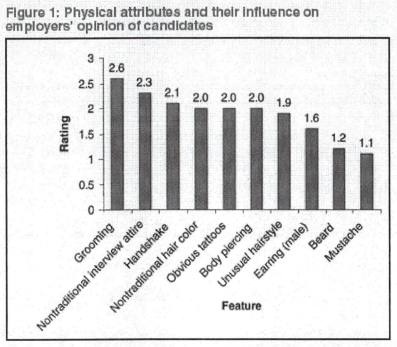

Figure 1: Physical attributes and their influence on employers' opinion of candidates

(3-point scale, where 1=no influence, 2=slight influence, and 3=strong influence)
Source: *Job Outlook 2001*, National Association of Colleges and Employers.

If your recruiter asked for anything in particular, make sure you have it with you. Off-campus interviews sometimes involve copies of your official transcripts, letters of recommendation, certificates, or documentation of special skills or talents you may have. A valise or briefcase may be helpful to carry some of these things. Most recruiters would not expect to see a backpack or book bag, though; that's the sort of thing a student would carry, but not a professional. Even though you are a student, you send the signal to your interviewer that you're ready to make the transition from school to the working world by dressing and behaving like a businessman or woman.

Greeting Skills

These things may seem very basic, but they're worth reviewing, just so you'll know what most professional corporate recruiters expect.

- Wait to be invited into the interview room. If you're told by a receptionist to go right in, simply knock twice, open the door and introduce yourself.

- Smile, be positive, be enthusiastic, and be energetic. It's one thing to be professional and businesslike; it's another to look like you're headed for a funeral.

- Don't sit down until you're invited to do so.

- Put your briefcase on the floor next to your chair. If your notepad is small, keep it in your lap. Under no circumstances should you put your briefcase, your notepad, your feet, or anything else on the interviewer's desk. That desk is semi-sacred territory; it belongs to the interviewer and not to you.

- If you're offered coffee or a soft drink, accept if you'd like some. If you're not interested, decline politely. Don't bring anything to eat or drink into the interview room with you. And, for heaven's sake, don't light a cigarette, cigar, or pipe during the course of an interview. Interviewers who smoke are rare, indeed. If you're offered a cigarette – even if you're a smoker – it would be wise to decline and wait until you're done with the interview and out the door to light up.

Nonverbal Skills

You communicate without using words just as effectively – or perhaps more so – than you do by speaking or writing during an interview.

- Sit up straight. Don't slouch or throw one arm over the back of the chair.

- If you cross your legs, do so in a demure, professional manner. Men should be just as careful of this as women. The typical "figure-4" position in which men rest one ankle on the other knee is regarded as most unprofessional.

- Make and maintain eye contact with the interviewer. It may be difficult to do, especially if you're unaccustomed to that sort of thing, but try your best to remain focused on the interviewer and what he or she is saying. Look directly at him or her as you respond to questions.

- Don't exhibit nervous mannerisms: thumb-twiddling, finger-drumming, toe tapping, knee-bouncing, and the like. Don't play with rubber bands, paper clips, pens, pencils, notepads, your necktie, your hair, or other artifacts and articles of clothing or jewelry.

- When the interviewer offers a hand to shake yours, reach out and take his or her hand firmly. No extremes, please. Limp-wristed handshakes or bone-crushing "gorilla grips" won't help you.

- Follow the interviewer's moves. When he or she stands to indicate the interview is over, stand up.

Listening Skills

Your ability to listen is a function of your willingness to practice the basics involved in human dialogue. And, without question, well-developed and frequently practiced listening skills will help you land the job you want. Recruiters and company representatives are especially looking for someone who can:

- Pay attention to what's going on;

- Follow a conversation, listening at some points and talking at others;

- Remember what's been said;

- Respond to the question that's just been asked;

- Recall in some detail during a second interview what you heard in your first interview.

- "Listen between the lines," paying attention not only to what's been said, but how it was said, and to what hasn't been said, as well.

Being on the Mark When You're on the Spot

Even the best prepared of job candidates can be at a loss for words when tough or unexpected questions arise. Here are a few that CNN.com's Larry Keller thinks you should be prepared for:

What are your weaknesses? You probably needn't mention that you have panic attacks under tight deadlines, but do answer honestly while at the same time emphasizing your strengths.

You can even make a weakness sound like a strength. You might say, for example, that you tend to take on too many responsibilities – then tell how you've taken steps to correct this.

Do you have any questions? If you answer "no," you seem uninterested or lacking enthusiasm for the job or the employer. But don't ask about company benefits, such as their 401(k) and health-care plans. Wait until you receive a job offer before you get into that. You might ask other questions about the company that weren't answered during the interview. For example, you might inquire about what areas of the company are undergoing change, or restructuring. You could ask about the company's corporate culture, or about company-sponsored programs for employees' volunteer work in the community.

Why do you want to leave your current job? A prospective employer wants to know that you're looking elsewhere because you're ambitious – you see greater challenges, a promotion, or new opportunity. So focus on your desire to assume more responsibility and to advance in your field.

Why should we hire you? Emphasize how your experience, education, and accomplishments in school and on the job make you a perfect fit for this company. Show how you can be an asset to the employer.

What do you think of your previous boss? This is an easy one if you like your last supervisor. If you don't, please refrain from saying so. There must be something you liked or respected about that person. Mention the positive quality rather than offering criticism.

Where do you want to be 10-or-15 years from now? You may not really know what you want to be doing so far in the future. But don't be afraid to talk about a desire to be the best in your chosen field, and about your interest in assuming greater responsibilities and developing expertise in more areas. All of this translates into making you a more valuable employment prospect.

What *Not* to Say in an Interview

If you're a smart job candidate, you've already thought about the points you want to make to sell yourself during an interview. Perhaps you've even practiced your pitch during a mock interview. That's good, of course, but know too that career experts caution that saying *too* much in an interview can hurt your prospects.

- Don't address your interviewer by his or her first name, unless and until it's clearly established that the session is on a first-name basis. Here, the rule is to let the interviewer speak first. If you're immediately called by your first name – and particularly if the handshake comes with, "Hi, I'm Alice" – then you know that first names are the order of the day. If you don't get such signals (yes, even in the Age of IT and pierced noses), stick to the more formal last-name approach.

- Don't use the wrong name, first or last.

- Don't say anything that conveys that you're desperate for the job, even if you are. "You want to appear there are other opportunities on your horizon," writes Robin Ryan in *60 Seconds & You're Hired* (Penguin USA, 2001). "You may have to act; maybe you *are* desperate. But if you convey that desperation to the employer in the interview, it can hurt your chances of getting hired."[xli]

- Don't bash your former boss or company. You'll be perceived as a malcontent and the person interviewing you will wonder if you'll rip your next employer, too.

- Don't ask, "What do you do here?" Again, research the company carefully, and where possible, the interviewer.

- Don't brag. Yes, you need to sell yourself by recounting your achievements, but do so by demonstrating the results of what you did. "Bragging often comes from weak candidates thinking they can snow the interviewer," Ryan writes. "Results, specifics, and examples with substance are what will really impress an employer."

- Don't be a windbag. If you ramble too long in your responses, your interviewer's mind may start to wander. Stay on point. Ryan recommends keeping responses to 60 seconds or less.[xlii]

Questions You Should Be Prepared to Answer

Here is a series of questions that is, for the most part, entirely reasonable. Look through this list and think about the answers you might give if an interviewer were to ask you about these subjects. If you don't have a good answer for each of them, work on them.

- How did you find out about this job?

- How are things going at school?

- Where were you born and raised?

- Why did you choose this major?

- What were your favorite subjects?

- Why did you attend this college or university?

- What extra-curriculars interest you?

- What clubs or organizations do you belong to or participate in?

- Do you have any military service?

- What do your parents do?

- Are you working now?

- How did you finance your education?

- Have you ever been fired? Why?

- What did you do during summers in college?

- Have you ever held a part-time job?

- Have you ever done volunteer work?

- What was the most interesting or satisfying job you've ever held? Why?

- Who was your best supervisor? Why did you like him or her the most?

- What is your recent salary history?

- What sort of person are you?

- What educational plans do you have?

- What are your most notable professional strengths?

- What are your most interesting personal qualities?

- How do you define or measure success?

- Where do you want to be five years from now? Ten years? Why?

- Do you prefer working alone or in teams?

- Do you like to travel?

- Tell me three things about yourself you don't like. What would you change?

- Tell me something about yourself you think very few people know.

- What do you know about our company?

Questions You Do *Not* Have to Answer . . . Unless You Want To

These are questions which are intrusive, excessively personal, and – in most cases – illegal. You may certainly decline to provide an answer, but you should do your best not to appear shocked if an interviewer should ask one or more of them.

- How old are you?

- Are you married? Are you engaged?

- Are you planning to have children?

- How would you describe your skin tone? That's an interesting name. What's your ethnic background?

- Have you ever been arrested? Have you ever been convicted of a felony? (This may be a requirement on certain state and federal employment applications.)

- Are there any misdemeanors that don't show up on your record?

- What's your religious affiliation? Do you attend church regularly? Do you donate time or money to your church?

71

- What's your credit history? Have you ever filed for bankruptcy?

- Have you ever had legal troubles? Ever been sued? Are there any outstanding judgments or liens against you?

- Any children or elderly relatives who are legally or financially dependent on you?

- Have you ever lied on an application? Cheated on your income tax?

- Where do your relatives work? How much do they make?

Handling Illegal or Unethical Questions

Dealing with questions that are clearly either illegal or unethical requires both patience and skill. Your objective is to find a job – that's why you agreed to be interviewed. If you challenge, confront, or threaten an employer, chances are not good that you'll be offered a position.

First, try to focus on the issue and not the question. The interviewer may simply have framed the question in a clumsy or inappropriate manner. You should respond to legitimate interests. If an employer wants to know, for example, why you're leaving your present job, you're obligated to explain that. If you've been fired or laid-off, you may wish to protect some of the details surrounding your last employer and your relationship with that firm, but you may also want to provide the interviewer with enough detail to satisfy his or her curiosity.

It's really up to you to decide for yourself what you can and must reveal. You can end an interview at any point if you decide the questions are inappropriate, rude, intrusive, or probe into areas that you don't want to discuss. A better strategy, however, might be to defer, deflect the question, or inquire about why the information is needed. If the interviewer responds with a legitimate use or need for the information, you may wish to reevaluate your reasons for withholding.

Your basic goal in such situations is to stay likeable. If the interviewer decides he doesn't like you, you're done for. If she should decide that you're being elusive or untruthful, you won't get the job. If you've really been abused by an interviewer, you can always contact your local Equal Employment Opportunity Commission to report the incident and ask for advice. As a last resort, you can obtain legal counsel and file suit against the firm for discriminatory employment practices. That will be expensive, time-consuming, and painful, of course, but it may provide you with some measure of satisfaction if you've been treated badly.

The interviewer is in charge of the interview, not you. Don't attempt to steer the conversation in directions you'd like to go; let him or her lead. You will almost always be offered an opportunity to add anything you'd like the interviewer to know toward the end of your time together. If there's something crucial you need to say about yourself or the job you're applying for, you'll have an opportunity to bring it up at that time.

Questions You Might Want to Ask

In addition to preparing responses for the various types of questions employers are likely to ask of you, here are a few questions you might wish to ask of them:

- What duties are involved in this position?

- Will the day-to-day responsibilities change with time?

- Is there a probation period? If so, how long is it?

- What is the starting date?

- What is the usual period of evaluation? How do you evaluate employees?

- What would you be willing to share with me about the company's strategic direction?

- What would my prospects for advancement be?

- Is there anything about the company's job-rotation, management development, or training programs that isn't included in the literature you sent me or on the company's Web site?

- How many people hold this sort of job in your firm? How long, on average, do they hold it?

- Sounds like a wonderful opportunity. What do you see as the disadvantages, risks, or challenges?

- Finally, as you head for the door, you may wish to ask how long you should expect to wait before you hear back from your interviewer about the next steps in the process.

Wrap-Up Skills

When the interview is over, the interviewer will let you know by standing up, thanking you for your time and interest in the company. Respond by thanking the interviewer for his or her time and interest in you. Tell the interviewer you would like an opportunity to learn more about the company and to meet other people in the organization, and that you hope to hear back from them before long. A confident, winning smile and a firm handshake should conclude your time together. Move to the door with him or her directly, but in a confident, professional manner. Don't forget your notebook, briefcase, or purse. Don't leave anything in the interview room.

CHAPTER 9

WHEN YOU'RE OFFERED A JOB

It will happen – sooner or later – you'll be offered a position with one of the firms that you've interviewed with. What do you do now? You really have three choices: you can accept, decline, or request an extension.

Accepting an Offer

Assuming you don't wish to further negotiate the details of a position, you should respond promptly and courteously to their offer. A letter of acceptance should contain three things: a direct and unambiguous sentence accepting the offer, a statement regarding when you intend to begin work, and an expression of thanks to the company for their confidence in you. You may wish to include change-of-contact data, if you're planning to move or will relocate shortly after graduation. Make sure your new employer knows how to reach you: by postal service, by telephone, and by e-mail.

Be certain that you are clear on whether an exchange of letters is sufficient to guarantee your new position, or whether you will be asked to sign an employment contract. If the latter is the case, you may wish to show it to an attorney or have a trusted senior advisor look through it and provide you with his or her best advice. If the contract is simple and fairly short, you should look through it yourself and, if you agree with the terms and are ready to accept, sign it directly. Your willingness to do so shows both self-confidence and an eagerness to begin work.

Declining an Offer

If you're sure you don't want to accept a particular job offer, you should write to the firm, declining the offer in direct, but polite terms. Similar to the acceptance letter, this letter should be unambiguous and clear about what you intend, but not abrupt or rude. You may cite an offer of employment elsewhere (without mentioning the company by name) as a reason for your declining their offer. You should also thank that firm for their confidence in you.

Above all else, you should do whatever you can to maintain a friendly working relationship with any firm you decline employment from. Keep in mind that, were it not for a better offer from another firm, you might be happily employed with this company. And, given an uncertain economy, mergers, buyouts, and other fluctuations – who knows? – you could be working for them before you know it. Remain on good terms and burn no bridges as you move to secure employment elsewhere.

Asking for an Extension

If you're not sure what to do about an offer, or if you're waiting to hear from someone else, you may want to write or call the company and ask for an extension. This request should be direct, polite and brief. Explain that you need an additional period of time (be specific: one week, ten days, two weeks, or thirty days) to decide whether or not to accept their offer. Explain that a brief extension will help you to make an informed and responsible decision, and that you appreciate their cooperation and understanding. An extension of two-to-three weeks is not uncommon in many employment situations, particularly with professional positions. Some firms may have specific training dates you'll be asked to meet or other special requirements you will want to inquire about.

As an ethical matter, you can *never* accept a position with one firm and then continue to look for work at others. If you accept an offer and then back out because you've found something better, you'll have done three things wrong: to begin with, you will have caused serious problems for the company that hired you in the first place. They thought they had a qualified, interested, and committed employee on board. Now, they're forced to continue their search. Second, you will create a bad name for your school and for other students or graduates who apply for employment with the firm you back away from. And, finally, you will create a bad name for yourself. Your reputation will follow you throughout your career and it's simply a terrible idea to establish a reputation as untrustworthy, unreliable, or deceptive before your career has even begun.

Negotiating the Terms of an Offer

First things first. You should never begin negotiating without an offer. If you try to influence anything from starting salary to vacation and benefits, you'll look greedy, self-centered, and very much like you're not a team player. Greed and avarice went out with the '90s. Team players are in again. Here are a few considerations as you think about what and how to negotiate with your new employer.

Ask for a few days to think it over. If you're certain you want this job, say yes and politely ask when you can expect to see an offer in writing. If you're not, ask for the offer in writing and then inquire about the consideration period. If your recruiter asks how long you need, be honest about it and say, "A few days." Or, specify a particular day on which you will contact the firm again.

Steer clear of the offer deadline. If you're hoping to negotiate a different training start-date or additional moving allowance, don't wait until the last minute. Do yourself and your prospective employer a huge favor and bring the discussions to closure well in advance of the deadline they've given you. If you wait until the last minute, your recruiter and prospective co-workers will think you've been shopping their offer around to other employers.

Be polite. This isn't a used car lot, nor is it a collective bargaining agreement with the Teamsters. Maintain your composure and stay cool about all of this. The advice is simple: be polite, professional, and persistent. Ask for what you think you really need and respond gracefully to the answer. You, and only you, must decide if close-in parking, extra vacation, or some other issue becomes a deal-breaker. How much do you want this job, and how badly do you want to work for this employer? Even if you ultimately walk out the door and don't accept the position, you want these people to think well of you. You'll need every ally in your career that you can make, and you may very well see these folks again before long.

Do your research. Before you walked into your first interview, you knew that you would stand very little chance of being hired if you didn't thoroughly research who they are, what they do, and which market space they compete in. The same holds true for salary. Do your best to be informed about what a company is likely to pay for the position you want. Peter Goodman, author of *Win-Win Career Negotiations* recommends visiting salary sites, including www.SalaryExpert.com, to research salaries for related positions at similar firms in similar regions.[xliii]

If you are pressed by a recruiter to provide a figure, you should consider offering a salary range based on your research. Most experts strongly recommend against offering a money figure first, but it's sometimes difficult to avoid. "Companies can't react to something they don't know," says Scott Stahlmann, a vice president for talent acquisition at Prudential Financial, Inc. In Newark, New Jersey. He argues that candidates could hurt their chances for a position by being coy about salary issues, and says he always asks candidates for their salary requirements in preliminary phone interviews. "The ones who don't give me an answer usually won't get a call back," he says.[xliv]

So what should you do if a recruiter asks how much money you're looking for? Most experts say you should wait until you have an offer of employment on the table. Sometimes a simple deferral will work: "I'm sure you compensate your managers fairly. I'm just looking for an opportunity to show you what I can do for your company." If that won't work, you might try this: "I'd rather wait until we've agreed on an offer of employment to begin talking about salary." On the one hand, you don't want to undersell yourself by asking for a low-ball salary, just hoping you'll get a job. And on the other, you don't want to price yourself out of the market by asking for a figure at the very top of the salary range for that position. Go into that second (or third) interview armed with current information about what such positions pay and be ready to negotiate in good faith.

Be reasonable. Some issues are simply not within the negotiating authority of the recruiter. If you're being hired for a particular position, for example, the starting salary may be determined by the position classification. Your experience, charm, and good looks will be insufficient to alter the company's willingness to reclassify the job. Other issues may be within the authority of the recruiter to negotiate. If salary is something she can't influence, how about asking for moving expenses or a "transition allowance" that will permit you to get your telephone and utilities hooked up and furniture out of storage? You may be able to influence your starting date or the start-date for training. You may be able to influence the date of your first performance review, leading to an early promotion or advancement. And, in some circumstances, you may be able to negotiate a performance-based bonus into your contract. Just like a major league baseball player, you might ask for additional compensation if you achieve certain specified performance outcomes during your first year or two on the job.

Be quiet. Don't feel compelled to dominate the conversation. If your recruiter makes you an offer, your best move may be to remain quiet for a few moments. If she really wants you to sign the contract today, she may feel the need to break that silence and raise the offer or respond to the issues that concern you most. As we just mentioned, be polite and be reasonable, but don't feel as if you must fill every lull in the conversation.

What If You Don't Hear from Them?

As we explained in Chapter 8, you should be prepared to ask your interviewer several different types of questions. As the interview wraps up, we suggested that you ask when you might expect to hear back from the company. Most interviewers will give you a quick response based on the number of people they're reviewing and the number of positions they have to fill. The initial screening period is usually not longer than ten days to two weeks.

But what if two or three weeks go by and you don't hear anything? Was the letter lost in the mail? Did your roommate delete the voice message? Is the e-mail server down? It's easy to panic when your anxiety level is high to begin with, but don't let your emotions control your response. Compare the calendar to your notes from the interview and give both the interviewer and the company the benefit of the doubt. If she said "ten days," give her 15. If he told you "two weeks," give him three.

Once you've allowed for a reasonable grace period and still haven't heard anything, begin with a brief e-mail message enquiring about the position. Use capital letters, a salutation and complimentary closing, as well as conventional spelling and punctuation. Your message might look something like this:

Dear Ms. Allen:

Thanks very much for spending some time with me on January 29th at the Campus Career Center. I enjoyed learning more about [your company] and was especially grateful to talk with you about the value I know I can bring to [your company's] marketing program.

I look forward to hearing from you again at your earliest convenience. You'll find me at 270-555-1212 during the day, and at 270-666-3434 evenings and weekends.

Sincerely,

Hunter McLemore

Once you've given your interviewer twice the time period she told you she would take before replying, you can safely pick up the telephone and call. Be polite, be professional, and be respectful of her time, but ask directly if she has any information for you regarding the outcome of your interview on January 29th. Most recruiters are notoriously difficult to reach by telephone, but persistence is a virtue you may wish to cultivate. Don't be annoying or pushy. Just demonstrate your interest – once again – in the position you spoke about and ask if she has any news to share with you.

Some recruiters, often associated with smaller or start-up firms, may lack the professionalism to call when they should. Some may ignore you entirely. After the e-mail, the phone call, and the second e-mail, you should consider writing a formal business letter. It will look much like the e-mail message, but will conclude with a statement about your continuing interest in the company and a polite thank-you for her time and interest in you. Sign it, mail it, and then begin working on your other contacts.

A Final Thought

Looking for work isn't easy, but it's not as daunting as many people imagine. It's likely that you'll find yourself switching jobs, moving from one company to another, or perhaps changing career paths several times before you're ready for retirement. Remember: the more you know about yourself and the more you know about what employers want and need, the easier the process will be. Best wishes as you begin your journey.

LOOKING FOR WORK AFTER GRADUATION:
One Woman's Story

"I was unemployed when I graduated from business school," said Kristin Potts, "but it wasn't because I hadn't tried to find a job. I worked like a maniac during my last semester of grad school, looking for work. And I'm convinced the reason I didn't find anything is because I took a shotgun approach to my job search. I didn't actually find what I wanted until I became much more focused."

Kristin Potts is now a Product Manager for Hollister, Inc., a privately-held, $500 million manufacturer of health care products in suburban Chicago. She's a graduate of California Polytechnic State University in San Luis Obispo, with a degree in marketing. "I went to work in banking right after graduation," she said, "but after four years of that, I decided that I didn't really want to be a banker. The work was good," she added, "but it just wasn't what I wanted to do for the rest of my life."

Potts returned to school to pursue an MBA through an accelerated business school program in the Midwest . "That year went by pretty fast," she recalled, "and by the time commencement rolled around, I still hadn't found anything and was beginning to panic." She thinks the reason she didn't find work the second time around is because she didn't understand the job search process.

"After an unbelievable number of rejections, I sat down and began to think seriously about what I wanted to do and where I wanted to do it. I began with a close look at who used the channels of distribution I was experienced with. One morning I walked through Wal-Mart and began reading the wrappers on candy bars to see who made them and where they were manufactured. Then I walked down the other aisles and looked at who made what sort of toy products, housewares, and so on. It was really an educational experience to see where some of those products come from."

The trip to Wal-Mart was informative, but not as useful as a trip to the Chicago Public Library. She started with *Crain's Chicago Business*, a weekly business publication focused on the city in which she wanted to work. "Their almanac issue lists the major firms in the city, categorized dozens of different ways: top firms owned by women, publicly-held firms, by industry, by location." Potts knew that she wanted to work for a manufacturer, so she began listing manufacturers around the Chicago area.

"After I had that list, I logged on to a data system called *Infotrack* – it was absolutely the best thing that happened to me since I had graduated," she said. "The online data system lists the corporations in each region of the country. It tells you who the officers are, who's on the board of directors; it gives you names, addresses, phone numbers – an incredible amount of detailed information that will help you get around the human resources people who'll just throw your resume in the trash. It helped me meet people and get to those people who actually do the hiring."

"*Infotrack* also provided a great deal of special information, including the characteristics of the firms and the products they manufacture," she added. "I used a lot of that information when I went for interviews, but I didn't stop there." The research for her job hunt took her to various retail outlets. "I was looking for a job at Florsheim, but the corporate data didn't tell me anything about their products, so I went into a Florsheim Shoe Store and talked with the manager for about an hour. He told me all about their principal competitors, their best products, and their product failures. He was incredibly helpful. When I interviewed with Florsheim, the recruiter was impressed with what I knew about the firm. I didn't get the job," she said, "but it was a great experience anyway."

How did she get the job she has now? "Despite my best efforts," she observed, "I got this job from an ad in the paper. Don't discount any opportunities or leads, especially when you know what you want." Her advice for finding a job once you've left school: "Don't force the fit because of a fear of unemployment. Make absolutely sure the fit between you and the job is right. When it is, you'll have a wonderful job that you'll want to keep."

Questions

1. What do you suppose Kristin learned from reading product package labels in Wal-Mart?

2. What sort of things could you learn from visiting a retail establishment or store, such as the Florsheim Shoe Store that Kristin visited? How should you prepare for such a visit?

3. Since she eventually found her current job through a newspaper advertisement, wasn't the rest of her job search really a waste of time and effort?

4. If looking for work is really a full-time job in itself, how can a student possibly do that during the last year of college or grad school?

5. What's wrong with a "shotgun approach" to a career search? If you mail out enough resumes, won't someone eventually see how talented and valuable you are?

6. What other sources are available in your library to help you find work?

THE RECRUITING PROCESS AT FORD MOTOR COMPANY

Recruiting new employees is a very competitive process, and no one knows it better than Bill Westhaus. "We're looking for the very best people we can hire. We want to interest them in Ford, and get them to think about working for Ford Motor Company. At the same time, the very best students out there are looking for the best jobs they can find. Our competitors, of course, are looking for the very same people."

Bill Westhaus is Manager of Strategic Planning and Analysis for the Continuous Improvement Recognition System at Ford Motor Company, and works at the company's world headquarters in Dearborn, Michigan. He's a Notre Dame graduate with an MBA from the Wharton School of Finance at the University of Pennsylvania. Ford Motor Company is the lowest-cost producer of domestic motor vehicles and the number-one producer of trucks in the United States. Ford is listed as the number 5 company on the *Fortune 500* list, with annual worldwide sales of $100 billion.

"Our annual recruiting process," said Westhaus, "begins with the establishment of quotas for hiring. In any one year, we may hire about 50 finance professionals who'll initially go to work in analysis, treasury, internal auditing, or accounting positions. The next step is to decide how many colleges and universities we'll visit. Since as many as half of our 50 new-hires may come from our summer intern program, we could be looking for only 25 additional people, so we'll probably visit no more than 20 campuses to search for those people."

"Our search will include a careful look at the diversity of the populations at various campuses," he said, "as well as the quality of the academic programs and the success of past graduates. We tend to be successful at Midwest and Big Ten schools, but we won't restrict our search to just those schools."

Westhaus acknowledged that the Career & Placement Centers on each campus play an important role in determining who gets an interview with Ford. "Half of our interviews are invitational and half are open. Students will bid for the open interviews on each campus, while we select those we'd like to talk to during the invitational interviews. Students submit resumes to the schools and they pass them on to us. We review them carefully and select those we'd like to interview."

How does a student get invited to an interview with Ford? "A well-prepared resume is the first step," said Westhaus. "You have to catch my eye in a quick, 30-second scan, and if the resume isn't first-class, you won't go any further." Even if a student isn't invited to interview, Westhaus recommends attending an evening reception prior to the interview date. "My associate, Sandy Ulsh, and I come to campus the night before the formal interviews and try to answer questions about Ford Motor Company and get a number of preliminary issues out of the way early. We try to answer all of those 'What's it like to work at Ford?' questions that evening."

Westhaus brings several people with him to deal with student curiosity. "I'm lead recruiter on these trips," he said, "and I'll bring two or three younger employees with me to interact with the students. They deal with work-related issues and typical new-hire questions. They also handle the meeting materials." Westhaus noted that all students are welcome, even though they may not have an invitation to interview. "Bring a resume, talk to us, and we'll take a look at your potential," he said.

Westhaus and Ulsh, who is Manager of Pricing and Financial Analysis in Ford's light truck operation, will each interview 13 candidates the next day. "I've done as many as 37 in three days," he said, "but that's just too much. We have to take careful notes to remember who each of these people are. This process is just too important for us to allow candidates to blur in our minds. It's just too expensive for Ford to make a mistake."

Westhaus and his colleague work from an interview form that has behaviorally-based questions that ask job applicants to describe how they performed under very specific circumstances in previous situations. The form contains what he describes as "thought-starters." "My specific questions usually come first, followed by some open-ended questions. I do try to change the order and pacing, though, because I know students talk to each other about the interviews."

Westhaus explained what he's looking for in a job applicant. "I explore specific job-related experience, team-related activities, and problem-solving they may have done," he said, "because we're looking for a very specific set of qualifications. Communication skills come high on our list. We want to know if the candidate can speak and interact confidently with others. Quantitative abilities are also high on the list, as are leadership, teamwork, and motivation."

"I'm usually most impressed with someone who's taken the time to find out something about Ford. If they know our product line, how we're organized, and what we do, it helps. Those who stand out have prepared by learning about us. In other words, it is clear that they *really* want to work for Ford Motor Company."

After the interviews, Westhaus and his associate will review their findings and rate the candidates. "We usually will find as many as five or six very desirable candidates out of our visit to a campus," he said, "and within 72 hours we'll review the results of the interviews with representatives of the locations within the company who do the hiring. Within a short time, they contact the candidates to extend invitations for second interviews, and I follow up within a week or 10 days by mail to confirm that."

"A second interview involves an entire day in one of our plants or operating locations, with seven or eight one-on-one encounters, lunch, and a location tour. We try to prepare the candidates with background information on the people they'll meet and the facility they'll tour. If we're favorably impressed, a job offer will come from the interviewing location." Westhaus acknowledged that it's a grueling and difficult process for many of the candidates, as well as the recruiters. "It's very important," he added, "that we find just the right people for the positions we know will be open. And all along the way, we're watching, listening, evaluating – searching for those clues that will tell us whether or not this is *the person* who'll be right for Ford."

Questions

1. Can you describe the process at your campus for obtaining an employment interview?

2. If you're not invited to interview with a particular company, but would genuinely like to work for them, what's the best way to approach that company?

3. What's the difference between an "informational interview" and an "employment interview?"

4. What sort of clues do you imagine Mr. Westhaus and his colleagues are looking for when they watch, listen, and examine job applicants?

5. Westhaus mentioned that he asks questions which are specifically related to past job experience, team-related activities, and problem solving. What if you've never held a full-time job before? How should you respond to such questions?

6. How would you *personally* show a recruiter such as Mr. Westhaus that you're confident, capable, and eager to work for a company like Ford?

THE ETHICS OF RESUMES AND RECOMMENDATIONS:
When do filler and fluff become deception and lies?

Jason Eckerle returned to his desk from lunch with a single mission in mind: to select the half-dozen best candidates for a regional customer service manager's position. As he hung up his suit jacket, Eckerle sized up the stack of resumes and recommendations he'd been dealing with all morning – more than a hundred of them.

The work had been slow but steady, gradually forming three distinct piles: one contained absolute rejects (not enough work experience, wrong academic credentials, poor recommendations from former employers). The second contained a few definite candidates for personal interviews, while the third held the applications of those about whom he still had questions or reservations.

His task for the afternoon – selecting three more applicants to bring to the company headquarters for interviews – was complicated by the resumes and recommendation letters themselves. Some questions were obvious: "This guy lists five years full-time sales and marketing experience, yet he's only 22 years old. How can he go to school full-time and have that kind of experience?" Here's another: "This young lady says she went to school at The Sorbonne in Paris for two years, yet on the application form, under the heading 'Foreign Languages,' she's checked 'none.'" Here's one more: "This fella says he has a degree from the University of Texas, yet nowhere on his resume does he say he lived or spent time there. Did he get that diploma by correspondence?"

Other issues are even more mysterious: "This young lady's resume lists education and work experience, but there's a three-year gap from 2001 to 2003. What's that all about? Is she trying to conceal something, or just absent-minded?" As Eckerle thumbed through another resume, he notices the application form declaring "fluency in Japanese, French, and Spanish." "How do you get to be *fluent* in a language unless you've lived where it's spoken?" he wondered. The resume didn't list any of those languages as native, nor did the applicant mention living abroad.

"Some of this stuff is outright fraud," he observed. As he sifted through the "reject" pile, Eckerle pulled out one application with an education entry that lists a degree the applicant didn't have. "When we checked," he said, "they told us he was close to finishing a master's degree, but he hadn't yet finished his thesis. The applicant said he had the degree in hand." Another listed work experience no one could verify. "This guy's resume says he was a client service representative for Litiplex, Inc. of Boston, but the phone book doesn't list any firms by that name, no one in our business has ever heard of them, and we can't check out his claims. I asked the applicant about the company, and he says, 'Maybe they went out of business.'"

Resumes weren't Eckerle's only problem. Recommendations were almost as bad. "Letters of recommendation aren't particularly useful," he said. "In the first place, almost no one is dumb enough to ask for a recommendation from someone who'll give them a bad one. Second, most recommenders write in broad, general, vague terms that don't tell me much about an applicant's work history, aptitude, or potential. They use glowing non-specific words that tell me the applicant's a marvelous human being, but don't say whether the guy's had any comparable work experience that I could use to help make a decision."

Eckerle mentioned one other recommendation problem. "Most of the people who write letters in support of a job applicant are fairly close friends of the applicant. They'll often say things that are laudatory, but just aren't true. By the time you're done reading the letter, you'd think the young man in question could walk on water. When he comes here for an interview, he can't get his own name straight." Excessive praise in letters of recommendation, Eckerle said, can be expensive for a firm when the recommendation just doesn't reflect the applicant's true potential. "It costs us nearly $2,000 to bring in an entry-level management candidate for interviews," he said, "and it's my job to make sure we don't bring in someone who's just not competitive." Inflated recommendations, he said, can make that job much more difficult.

Questions

1. Is a job applicant obligated to list *all employment* or *every work experience* on a resume? What about jobs in which an applicant has had a bad relationship with a supervisor? Is it fair to "load up" a resume only with positive work experience?

2. What if an applicant has been fired? Is a resume *required* to reveal the exact circumstances under which he or she left the job?

3. Is it ethical to list educational institutions or degree programs that an applicant has attended but not completed? How much detail is necessary? Should an applicant explain *why* he or she left a degree program or school without finishing?

4. Is a job applicant *obliged* to list offenses against the law on a resume? What about convictions or incarceration – say 30 days jail time for DWI?

5. Under such resume categories as "Foreign Languages," how does an applicant determine whether he or she is "fluent," "conversant," or merely "familiar with" a language? Do the same general rules apply to listing technical skills, such as computer languages and software applications?

6. In a letter of recommendation, is it ethical to lavish praise on a young man or woman, just because you know they're in need of a job? Conversely, does faint praise mean that a job applicant will likely be refused?

7. Is it better to turn away someone asking for a letter of recommendation, or should you do what's *honest* and tell a potential employer exactly what you think of the person?

8. Is a resume something like a *certificate of authenticity*, listing specifics and details with absolute adherence to honesty and accuracy, or is it more like a *sales brochure*, offering the best possible picture of a person in search of employment?

9. How well do you have to know someone before you can write an authentic, honest letter of recommendation? Is there a minimum time requirement before you can do so in good conscience?

10. Is the author of a letter of recommendation required to reveal *everything relevant* that he or she knows about an applicant? What about character or integrity flaws that may stand in the way of a job applicant's success? To whom is the author of such letters obligated? To the potential employer, or to the applicant?

REFERENCES

i. "Personal Essay," Northwestern University Graduate School. Retrieved on January 7, 2003 from http://www.northwestern.edu/graduate-fellowships/peressay.html.

ii. Ibid.

iii. For more detailed advice on beginning your essay, you may wish to consult Asher, D. *Graduate Admissions Essays: What Works, What Doesn't, and Why.* Berkeley, CA: Ten Speed Press, 1991. See also, Steltzer, R.R. *How to Write a Winning Personal Statement.* New Jersey: Peterson, 1991.

iv. Asher, D., pp. 46-47.

v. Personal Statement, graduate business school application of Arianne R. Westby. Used by permission.

vi. Ellin, A., "The Humble Resume Enters Cyberspace," *The New York Times*, Tuesday, January 30, 2001, p. E2.

vii. Bing, S., "How Not to Succeed in Business," *Fortune*, December 30, 2002, p. 210.

viii. "Padding of Resume Causes Bonus Loss," *The New York Times*, Thursday, October 31, 2002, p. C5. See also, Wayne, L., "Bausch & Lomb Executive Admits to Falsified Resume," *The New York Times*, Saturday, October 19, 2002, p. B2.

ix. "RadioShack's CEO Resigns Over Resume," *CBS News.com*, Tuesday, February 21, 2006. Retrieved from http://www.cbsnews.com/stories/2006/02/20/business.html.

x. Brooks, R., "MCG Capital CEO Takes Hit to Credibility Over Credentials," *The Wall Street Journal*, Monday, November 4, 2002, p. B2.

xi. Stanton, E., "If a Resume Lies, Truth Can Loom Large," *The New York Times*, Sunday, December 29, 2002, p. BU8.

xii. Ibid.

xiii. Tullier, L. M. And L. I. Lishing. *Cover Letters.* New York: NY: Random House / Princeton Review Books (1997).

xiv. Monin, L. *Every Woman's Essential Job Hunting & Resume Book.* Avon, MA: Adams Media Corporation (1994).

xv. Krannich, R. L. and C. R. Krannich. *201 Dynamite Job Search Letters*, 4th ed. Manassas Park, VA: Impact Publications (2001).

xvi. Goodwin, W., human resources manager, Bayer Corporation, Pittsburgh, PA. Telephone interview, May 7, 1996.

xvii. Maher, K., "Wanted: Ethical Employers," *The Wall Street Journal*, Tuesday, July 9, 2002, p. B7.

xviii. Ibid.

xix. Trevino, L. and K. Nelson. *Managing Business Ethics*, 3rd ed. New York, NY: John Wiley, Inc. (2003).

xx. Mullins, K., Monster.com public relations. Telephone interview, January 8, 2003. Follow-on data from ComScore Media Matrix: http://www.factmonster.com/ipka/A077993.html. Retrieved on Tuesday, March 7, 2006 at 3:03 p.m.

xxi. ComScore MediaMatrix, Reston, Virginia. Retrieved from http://www.comscore.com on Tuesday, March 7, 2006 at 2:54 p.m.

xxii. Murphy, A., Job.com director of sales and marketing operations. Telephone interview, January 9, 2003.

xxiii. Christopher, J. M.. Telephone interview, April 1995.

xxiv. Switzer, B. Telephone interview, April 1995.

xxv. Langford, L. Telephone interview, September 1995.

xxvi. Achilles, S. Telephone interview, September 1995.

xxvii. Wigton, K., Personal interview, September 1999.

xxviii. Lillibridge, L., Telephone interview, April 1995.

xxix. Hamil-Bajac, S., Telephone interview, April 1995.

xxx. Ibid.

xxxi. Christopher, J. M. Telephone interview, April 1995.

xxxii. Switzer, B. Telephone interview, April 1995.

xxxiii. Langford, L. Telephone interview, September 1995.

xxxiv. Peterson, M. Telephone interview, April 1995.

xxxv. Gallo, C. "Leaders Must Look the Part," BusinessWeek online. Retrieved on Friday, January 20, 2006 at 3:12 p.m. from http://www.businessweek.com.

xxxvi. Needleman, S., "Be Prepared When Opportunity Calls: Job Interviews by Phone Are No Less Formal Than Face-to-Face Meetings." *The Wall Street Journal*, Tuesday, February 7, 2006, p. B4.

xxxvii. Ibid.

xxxviii. Ibid.

xxxix. Bain and Company. Retrieved from www.bain.com/bainweb/join/interview on Tuesday, December 31, 2002 at 3:02 p.m. Reprinted by permission.

xl. Monster.com *Interview Center*. Retrieved from http://www.monster.com on Monday, December 30, 2002 at 9:45 p.m. Used by permission.

xli. Ryan, R. *60 Seconds & You're Hired*. New York: Penguin USA (2001).

xlii. Ibid.

xliii. Maher, K., "The Jungle: Focus on Recruitment, Pay, and Getting Ahead," *The Wall Street Journal*, Tuesday, December 24, 2002, p. B4.

xliv. Ibid.

APPENDIX A

Letters of Application

Cover Letters

September 29, 2005

MBA Recruiters
Global Corporate & Investment Banking
Bank of America Corporation
100 North Tryon Street
Charlotte, NC 28255

Dear MBA Recruiter:

I had a wonderful trip to New York last week and was very fortunate to talk with a few people from Bank of America. I am excited about the recent breakthrough news that Bank of America has acquired 10% of China Construction Bank's equity and hope that I can work for B of A to bring more of this kind of exciting news to the company in the future.

Bank of America, as one of the most important correspondent banks of my former employer, Industrial and Commercial Bank of China, actually is no stranger to me at all. I worked for ICBC for over ten years, learning about the full lines of international banking business, including international clearing and settlement, trade finance, foreign exchange transaction, and more. A fairly long tenure in the banking business also helped me to establish a solid network with my peers in other central banks in China, as well as commercial banks.

As a CFA Level II candidate and an MBA candidate focusing on finance, I am well prepared to devote myself to the banking industry in my future career. To prepare for that, I have gathered in-depth knowledge about accounting, financial management, equity valuation, and fixed income securities. I have excellent quantitative skills and interpersonal skills. I prefer to work in teams focused on the institutional financial market and will bring my strengths to such a position.

I would like to meet with you to talk further about my qualifications. Please do not hesitate to contact me at 574-514-2357 or xwang14@nd.edu.

Best regards,

Kathy Xiao Wang
MBA Candidate
Class of 2006

September 18, 2005

814 Coronation Gardens
South Bend, IN 46637

Ms. Kerry Daly
388 Greenwich Street, 37th Floor
New York, NY 10013

Dear Ms. Daly:

I am writing to you in reference to the Citigroup investment banking financial analyst position. I learned of this opportunity at your information session on campus and investigated it further on your website. What especially attracted me to working for Citigroup was the aggressive culture of the firm that would challenge me and provide for an environment where I could learn more every day.

As an analyst in my Applied Investment Management class, I am responsible for assisting in managing a $3.2 million class portfolio that serves as a part of Notre Dame's endowment. For my stock, the Tribune Company, I have performed extensive analysis focused on the company fundamentals, earnings forecast, valuation, and industry. I am confident that this experience and the skills developed from working in extensive detail on company specific reports, building financial models, and making presentations on the material will translate well to an investment banking position with Citigroup where work on deals would require many of the same skills. Furthermore, I have spent the past two summers interning in public audit at Ernst & Young and internal audit at Cedar Fair, L.P. My experiences at these firms provided me the opportunity to view companies from a unique perspective unavailable to external observers that helped to shape the way I think about analyzing companies. In addition, these experiences improved my communication skills as I had to interact with senior staff and management on a daily basis as well. Finally, I have a sincere interest in investment banking and can think of no more challenging, dynamic, and exciting of a career than helping to move the capital markets.

I would like the opportunity to further discuss my qualifications and passion for investment banking with you in an interview when you come to campus on September 27th. If there is anything else that I can do to assist you in this application process, please do not hesitate to contact me. Thank you very much for your consideration of me for a position with Citigroup, and I truly hope to hear back from you soon.

Sincerely,

Scott Soracoe

September 19, 2005

1503 N. Oakhill
South Bend, IN 46637

Ms. Anne Williamson
Associate Recruiting
The Boston Consulting Group
200 South Wacker Drive
Chicago, IL 60606

Dear Ms. Williamson:

After visiting The Boston Consulting Group Chicago office and speaking with numerous associates and consultants, I am very interested and excited about the associate position at your firm. I am particularly impressed with the diamond structure of the functional consulting groups and the breadth of expertise areas covered by BCG. The knowledgeable associates and consultants I spoke with conveyed the extraordinary culture of BCG.

As an entrepreneur, I have dealt with many issues including strategic planning, financing, employee relations, and marketing. Through my experiences as a multi-business owner and Director of Operations of the University of Notre Dame's Student Union Board, I have honed my leadership and communication skills. As Director of Operations, I have lead my team in implementing a new attendance policy, an incentive-based rewards program, and an interactive member directory. These improvements have aided in office efficiency and morale improvement. I am confidant that my experiences in business, academics and community service have created problem solving and analytical skills that will add value to your team.

Attached is my resume for your review. I have also e-mailed you my unofficial transcript and SAT / ACT scores. Thank you for all the opportunities you have given me to learn about BCG and the people who work for the organization. I would like the opportunity to further discuss my qualifications for the analyst position. I look forward to speaking with you. Thank you in advance for your consideration.

Sincerely,

Charles A Bassett II

January 9, 2006

348 Welsh Family Hall
University of Notre Dame
Notre Dame, IN 46556

Mr. Philip A. Laskawy
Managing Partner
Ernst & Young LLP
501 West Broadway, Suite 1100
San Diego, CA 92010

Dear Mr. Laskawy:

I recently spoke with Ms. Kelly Singer regarding internship opportunities with Ernst & Young.
and she suggested that I contact you. Ernst & Young's Assurance and Advisory Business
Services program is particularly impressive and would provide an excellent opportunity for me to
work directly with clients. I am very interested in a summer accounting position with your firm
and have enclosed my resume for your review.

As an accounting major at the University of Notre Dame, I have completed courses in audit
procedures and concepts. As my resume details, I have the basic skills and procedural
knowledge to be a valuable asset to your office this summer. Last year, I worked in a large,
managerial accounting department and became familiar with accounts payable, budgets, and
monthly financial statements. With my educational background and internship experience in
accounting, I know I'm ready for the next step.

I would like an opportunity to further discuss with you my qualifications and any employment
opportunities with Ernst & Young, LLP. I will call your office during the week of January 15th to
see if we can schedule a convenient time for a telephone interview. I look forward to speaking
with you.

Sincerely,

Debra Keim

Marissa Moschel

157 Cavanaugh Hall
Notre Dame, IN 46556
574-634-1403
Moschel.2@nd.edu

January 30, 2006

Jerrell Gaddis
Staffing Specialist / Internship Program Manager
9605 SW Nimbus
Beaverton, OR 97076

Dear Mr. Gaddis:

I am interested in applying for your summer internship in the area of Brand Marketing. I am currently a junior at the University of Notre Dame and am devoted to spending this summer learning more about different career paths in Marketing/Advertising. Your internship in Brand Marketing seems like a great fit with my interests and I have enclosed my resume for your review.

I have had experience working for a retail company, Abercrombie and Fitch, during my time here at Notre Dame. This experience has helped me to form a desired career path and understand the role of Marketing for a company. Abercrombie has had numerous problems with their risque advertisements and this has given me an unique perspective into the important role of Brand Marketing. I have also been very involved in organized athletics since a young age and continue to understand the importance of an active lifestyle. I am interested in pursuing a career in fashion and see Adidas as a perfect way to incorporate both of these interests.

Adidas now outfits all Notre Dame athletic teams and it would be interesting to apply what I have learned during an internship to what happens with athletics here at Notre Dame. I hope to develop a relationship with Adidas that will allow me to apply my skills of organization, persistence, and leadership while continuing to be involved in athletics.

I would enjoy the opportunity to learn more about Brand Marketing of athletic apparel and further my interests with Adidas. I look forward to hearing from you. Please feel free to contact me at Moschel.2@nd.edu or at 574-634-1403. Thank you for your consideration.

Sincerely,

Marissa Moschel

Enclosure: Resume

N'gomo Edwin Otiato   1818 Georgian Ct., South Bend, IN 46614
                                                             (574) 904-9383

_____

September 23, 2005

Bank of America
100 North Tyron Street
Charlotte, NC 28255

Dear MBA Recruiter:

Please consider my enclosed resume for the Global Corporate and Investment Banking Associate
position at Bank of America. Currently, I am a One-Year MBA student a the University of Notre
Dame Mendoza College of Business with a corporate finance concentration. The skills have I
have to offer Bank of America in this position include:

- **Self-driven achiever with strategic and creative thinking:** While working at
  Kenya College of Accountancy I strategically helped put in place a computerized
  accounting system that would help track down student account balances. This
  system was accurate, efficient, and cost effective, saving the college over
  $250,000 a year.

- **Demonstrated leader and team-focused player capable of building
  relationships:** I successfully headed the team that put in place the computerized
  accounting system at Kenya College of Accountancy. As the team head, I was
  specially charged with the duty of building a smooth, cordial, team relationship
  among the members.

- **Excellent quantitative and analytic abilities:** In order to confidently identify the
  independent living skills needed by the clients served at Dungarvin Inc and
  Indiana-Mentor Inc, I analyzed in depth their strengths and weaknesses. Based on
  the needs arising from the analysis and the budget allocation, I set up a training
  program that was in tandem with the needs in question. The program achieved
  remarkable results with at least 10 clients.

Bank of America is a global financial leader that offers client-focused solutions and leads in U.S.
corporate banking relationships. It serves 97% of the *Fortune 500* companies and has offices in
31 countries worldwide. I am committed to adding value and contributing to Bank of America's
expansion. Please consider placing me in your interview schedule during October.

Sincerely,

N'gomo Edwin Otiato

September 15, 2005

1650 Turtle Creek Court
South Bend, IN 46637

Ms. Gabriella Dalmolin
PricewaterhouseCoopers, LLP – Financial Advisory Services
200 E. Randolph, 74th Floor
Chicago, IL 60601

Dear Ms. Dalmolin:

I am a senior Finance major and Accountancy minor at the University of Notre Dame. I write to express my desire to be considered for a full-time position with the Financial Advisory Services division of PricewaterhouseCoopers.

I am particularly interested in both Business Recovery Services and Dispute Analysis and Investigations. I discovered these areas of FAS at the September 5th information session on campus, where I found myself attracted to the PwC philosophies of work-life balance and teamwork, as well as the personalities and attitudes of the employees who made the visit. I believe that my success in the quantitative coursework I have completed, as well as the actual experience I gained working in financial services at Merrill Lynch last summer have prepared me to step up to the type of exciting, challenging career which PricewaterhouseCoopers offers.

I have included my resume for your review, and am available to provide any other information needed at 574-271-6844 or at reiff.2@nd.edu. Thank you, Ms. Dalmolin, for your time and consideration. I look forward to speaking with you soon.

Sincerely,

Tobin J. Reiff

Enclosure: Resume

September 29, 2005

5818 Winamac Lake Drive
Apartment 1B
Mishawaka, IN 46545
574-274-4793
srubano@mac.com

Hiring Manager
Bank of America Corporation
100 North Tryon Street
Charlotte, NC 28255

Dear Hiring Manager:

I will be graduating with a Master of Business Administration degree in finance and am looking for a full-time position in the investment banking field. I am extremely interested in beginning my career at Bank of America. The investing history of Bank of America, especially its growth during the late 1990s has always amazed me.

I feel I have much to offer in B of A's drive to involve a younger generation of investors. As a Fixed Income Trader of the CSFB in Caracas, I managed the trading accounts of 31 individuals, making 12 percent annual returns over a three-year period. I have also obtained scholarships to pay for my MBA program, as I sustain a 3.8 grade point average in my field. I want to apply that vision and multitasking ability at Bank of America.

Bank of America is my first choice for entry into the professional arena after these years of hard work and late nights, and I believe that my employment would be highly beneficial to Bank of America, as well.

Thank you for your time and consideration. I look forward to discussing with you the ways I can contribute to B of A's future. You may reach me at 574-274-4793 or via e-mail at srubano@mac.com.

Sincerely,

Sebastian Rubano

Brenda A. Sullivan

2005 Coachmans Trail
South Bend, IN 46637
574-247-1658
Sullovan.186@nd.edu

January 31, 2006

Mr. John LaSage
Chairman, Central Region
Burson-Marsteller
233 North Michigan Avenue
Chicago, IL 60601

Dear Mr. LaSage:

I am currently a first-year MBA student at the University of Notre Dame. Professor James S. O'Rourke encouraged me to contact you concerning employment opportunities with Burson-Marsteller for this coming summer.

Before coming to Notre Dame, I spent four years as an Account Representative in the Marine and Energy Division at Marsh & McLennan Companies, Inc. Serving clients within the marine, petrochemical, and utility industries, I worked to identify and protect the insurance needs of their businesses. Client contacts, financial analysis, and site visits enabled me to thoroughly understand and assess a company's operations.

Professor O'Rourke has made it clear that experience in precisely the broad-based agency work that Burson-Marsteller offers, from crisis management to investor relations, would be an ideal summer experience for me as a first-year MBA student. My current and future coursework in communications, complemented by four years of work experience in a setting that emphasized client service, leads me to believe that Professor O'Rourke is correct.

I would welcome the opportunity to discuss Burson-Marsteller's practice and any potential employment opportunities. I have enclosed a copy of my resume for your consideration.

Sincerely,

Brenda A. Sullivan

Enclosure

Appendix B

Thank-You Letters

Letters of Acceptance

March 3, 2006

424 North Frances Street, Apr. #21
South Bend, IN 46617
Telephone: (574) 246-0716

Ms. Meg Lobus
The Sporting News
1935 Techny Road, Suite 18
Northbrook, IL 60062

Dear Ms. Lobus:

Thank you for the opportunity to interview with *The Sporting News* for a position in your
newsroom as a Staff Writer/Reporter. I enjoyed meeting you and learning more about your
company and my interest in working for your magazine remains strong.

I am confident that I have the necessary skills to succeed on your staff and to make an impact on
the magazine. In addition to my extensive coursework in which I have gained invaluable writing
experience, I have acquired a firm background in leadership and team-oriented skills from my
previous work experiences. I believe these skills to be essential in a team-based organization
such as a magazine.

Thank you again for the opportunity to meet with you. If you have any further questions, please
do not hesitate to contact me by telephone or e-mail. I look forward to hearing from you soon.

Sincerely,

Mark A. Overmann
movermann@nd.edu

February 10, 2006

181188-F Stone Ridge Street
South Bend, IN 46637

Mr. Michael Keane
Manager, Leader Identification and Sourcing
Whirlpool Corporation
Administration Center
2000 M-63 (Mail Drop 8523)
Benton Harbor, MI 49022-2692

Dear Mr. Keane:

Thank you for the opportunity to interview with the Whirlpool Corporation for a position in your Global Management Development Program. I am very excited about this opportunity and want to reaffirm my strong interest.

I enjoyed your presentation and the interview with Marcus Jones. I appreciate the time both of you took to explain the various responsibilities required by the position. I am confident that my communication skills, quantitative abilities, and leadership potential would make me an asset to Whirlpool Corporation.

Thank you for the opportunity to meet with you. I appreciate your hospitality and look forward to hearing from you.

Sincerely,

J. Elliot Aldrich

November 13, 2005

Benjamin Eichorn Blank
128B O'Neill Family Hall
University of Notre Dame
Notre Dame, IN 46556

Michael Sanders
White House Intern Coordinator
The Office of Management and Administration
Fax: 202-456-7966

Dear Mr. Sanders:

Thank you for extending first- and second-round interviews for an internship in the White House. I appreciate the opportunity to express my qualifications for the position. Having participated in the primary interview, I eagerly await another opportunity to convey my interests in seeking an internship.

During the second semester of my sophomore year at the University of Notre Dame, I traveled to Tokyo, Japan to study Japanese government and economics at Sophia University. Because the school years in Japan and the United States do not coincide, I did not receive an official copy of my Sophia University transcript until earlier this week. Notre Dame has now recorded the grades I received in Japan and updated my university transcript. Therefore, I wanted to inform the White House of my GPA from last semester, both at Sophia and at Notre Dame. An updated version of my transcript is on its way to you. A new copy of my resume is enclosed.

Thank you for considering these updates to my application. I look forward to the second-round interview on November 22 with Susan Ralston.

Sincerely,

Benjamin Eichorn Blank

September 20, 2005

University of Notre Dame
822 Pasquerilla East Hall
Notre Dame, IN 46556
(574) 634-0740

Allison Begg
PNC College Relations
Two PNC Plaza, P2-PTPP-20-4
Pittsburgh, PA 15222-2719

Dear Ms. Begg:

I would like to thank you for taking the time to discuss PNC's internship opportunities with me during your recent trip to Notre Dame. Through our discussion, not only did I learn more about the various requirements of the position, but I also sensed the strong dedication PNC has to its interns and the experience you create for them. This made a valuable impression on me and left me enthusiastic about the possibilities that lie ahead.

Confident that my communication and finance skills would allow me to significantly contribute to PNC's internship program, I want to reaffirm my strong interest in this position. If possible, I would like to arrange a brief interview in the near future to discuss in greater depth the rotations included in the internship.

Once again, that you for your time, insight, and consideration of my request. I will contact your office next week to schedule a short meeting so we are able to continue our discussion.

Sincerely,

Ellen Blystone
Blystone.1@nd.edu

Enclosure: Resume

Timothy D. Chase

307 East LaSalle Avenue, #336L
South Bend, Indiana 46617
(574) 251-0572
tchase@nd.edu

March 7, 2006

Mr. Harvey W. Griesman
Vice President
IBM Global Services
Route 100
Somers, NY 10589

Dear Mr. Griesman:

Thank you for speaking with me on the telephone yesterday about career opportunities at IBM. I particularly enjoyed learning about recent restructuring and new strategic initiatives in the company.

As I mentioned to you, before coming to Notre Dame, I served in a variety of capacities related to information systems and technology. As a consultant for Protiviti, I executed a variety of consulting projects related to improving business processes through current state analysis, process optimization, and incorporation of improved technology into business functions. In addition, I served as the lead consultant for the New Haven office's Enterprise Security group. This position enabled me to match client needs to the various security services we offered. Our projects successfully identified security exposures for our clients and provided them with an implementation plan to mitigate these risks.

I look forward to hearing from you again as interview season for internships draws near. If you need updated information about my professional experiences, activities, or classroom work, please contact me at any time via e-mail or telephone. In response to your instructions, I am enclosing a copy of my resume for your review.

Sincerely,

Timothy D. Chase

September 25, 2005

1540 North Oak Hill drive
South Bend, IN 46637
574-277-9095
ecummings.3@nd.edu

Mr. James Penman
Managing Director
Donnelly, Penman, French, Haggarty & Company
300 River Place, Suite 4950
Detroit, MI 48207

Dear Mr. Penman:

Thank you for considering me for the Investment Banking Associate position and for taking the time to meet with me last Thursday. I enjoyed learning about how someone like myself with an automotive background and Corporate Finance concentration can positively affect Donnelly, Penman, French, Haggarty & Company.

As I mentioned in the interview, my previous work experience as an analyst with various tier-one automotive suppliers, combined with my coursework at the University of Notre Dame, have prepared me to make a smooth transition into this position. My analytic and quantitative skills have been enhanced with each position in my career at Hella, Textron, and TRW. Similarly, my business school courses in corporate finance have provided me with a thorough understanding of the principles of finance. I am confident in my ability to make a valuable contribution to your firm.

I enjoyed our discussion about current trends within the investment banking community and, more specifically, in the automotive industry. I look forward to hearing from you later this week. In the interim, if you need additional information of any sort, please contact me via phone or e-mail. You have an electronic copy of my resume. A paper copy is enclosed.

Sincerely,

Edwin F. Cummings III

March 9, 2006

107 Sorin Hall
Notre Dame, IN 46556
574.634.2289

Mr. William Harrington
Pricewaterhouse Coopers, LLP
200 East Randolph Drive
Chicago, IL 60601

Dear Mr. Harrington:

It was a pleasure to meet you during your recent trip to Notre Dame. Thank you for giving me the opportunity to learn more about PricewaterhouseCoopers and the services that you offer. I feel fortunate to have the perspective of someone who is experienced, successful, and under forty. I left our meeting excited about the possibilities that lie ahead.

I am confident that I have the necessary qualifications to succeed in your organization. In addition to a strong academic background, I offer a practical background based on my leadership and previous work experience. This, I gathered, is essential in a team-based organization such as yours.

Thank you, again, for your time and insight. If you have further questions, please do not hesitate to contact me. I look forward to hearing from you soon.

Sincerely,

J. Lane Ewing

February 21, 2006

238 Howard Hall
Notre Dame, IN 46556
(574) 634-2551
jlapas@nd.edu

Mr. David Willie
Director, Human Resources
Hewitt Associates, LLC
100 Half Day Road
Lincolnshire, IL 60069

Dear Mr. Willie:

Thank you very much for meeting with me last week. As I said before, I am very interested in continuing with the selection process for a full-time position with Hewitt Associates.

I found our discussion about what an actuarial consultant does to be very helpful. I believe this job would fit well with my personality and skill set.

I hope you were pleased with my interview, and I hope to hear from you soon. Please contact me if you have any questions or need additional information.

Sincerely,

Jennifer Lapas

January 7, 2006

2250 North Cleveland Road
Apartment 1-F
South Bend, IN 46546
Telephone: 574/273-1569

Mr. William A. Westhaus
Manager, Early Career Development
Finance Personnel
Ford Motor Company
Room 828 WHQ
The American Road
Dearborne, MI 48121

Dear Mr. Westhaus:

I am pleased to accept your offer of a position as an entry-level finance manager with Ford Motor Company at a salary of $82,500 a year.

Your request that I report to Ford Headquarters on June 21, 2003 sounds fine to me. I will graduate from the University of Notre Dame on May 17th of this year and will be in Dearborne ahead of schedule, ready for work.

I appreciate Ford Motor Company's confidence in me and look forward to an exciting and rewarding future in the automotive industry.

Sincerely,

Todd Makenzie

APPENDIX C

Undergraduate Resumes

SCOTT J. SORACOE

ssoracoe@nd.edu

814 Coronation Gardens   1314 Rice Avenue
South Bend, IN 46637   Baltimore, MD 21228
C: 410-925-6598   H: 410-788-4771

OBJECTIVE: To obtain a full time position in investment banking.

EDUCATION: **University of Notre Dame**, Notre Dame, IN
Bachelor of Business Administration May 2006
Major: Finance, Major GPA: 3.78, Overall GPA: 3.71

Notre Dame London Program, London, England
Spring 2005 Study Abroad Program, GPA: 3.91
Completed Certificate of International Business

EXPERIENCE: **Applied Investment Management Class XXI**   Notre Dame, IN
Analyst   Fall 2005
• Assisted in managing $3.1 million portfolio that is part of University endowment
• Performed extensive stock specific analysis focused on the company background, fundamentals, earnings forecast, and industry

Ernst & Young   Baltimore, MD
Audit Intern   Summer 2005
• Worked as a member of teams performing quarterly/annual audit procedures and Sarbanes-Oxley 404 worksteps for multiple clients
• Performed additional work for clients associated with equity offerings, debt covenants, option reconciliations, and fixed asset checks
• Received extensive audit training through classroom and internet based sessions exploring the firm's global methodology, technology, and culture

Wachovia Securities   Baltimore, MD
Broker's Assistant   Winter 2004-2005
• Assisted in financial planning sessions with clients
• Implemented a strategic marketing campaign using the broker's database

Cedar Fair L.P.   Sandusky, OH
Internal Auditor   Summer 2004
• Worked extensively in documenting the purchasing, receipt, and transfer of inventory at Cedar Point for the Sarbanes-Oxley 404 bill
• Demonstrated written and verbal communication skills in every day interactions with upper and middle level management, park employees, and park guests

ACTIVITIES: *Member*, Student International Business Council - Finance Division
    GTCR Golder Rauner Leveraged Buyout Project 2004
    Credit Suisse First Boston Equity Analysis Project 2003
Mentor, Big Brother Program 2004-2005
Participant, North Central Trail Marathon 2003

HONORS: Dean's List: Spring 2005, Fall 2004, Fall 2003, and Spring 2003
NSCAA Adidas High School Scholar All-American 2002

SKILLS: Computer: Word, Excel, Access, PowerPoint, DreamWeaver

Anthony Gill

Permanent Address:
993 Whitney Lane SW
Rochester, MN 55902

Current Address:
1724 Turtle Creek Drive, Apt. 8
Notre Dame, IN 46637
(574) 514-4460

agill1@nd.edu

Objective: To obtain a full- time sales position applying my analytical and leadership skills.

Education: **University of Notre Dame** Notre Dame, IN
Bachelor of Business Administration, May 2006
Major: Marketing

Notre Dame London Program London, England
Summer 2004

Honors: Blue Collar Award, University Directories, Summer 2005
Number One Sales Team, University Directories, Summer 2005
NCAA Hockey Championship Participant, 2004
Most Dedicated Player Award, Cedar Rapid Rough Riders, 2000-2001, 2001-2002

Experience: **University of Notre Dame Varsity Hockey Team**   Notre Dame, IN
Participant   2002-Present
• Utilize team-building skills on a daily basis
• Understand the importance of preparation and time-management
• Motivate others by displaying dedication

WNDU – South Bend NBC Affiliate   South Bend, IN
Sports Journalism Internship   Scheduled to begin in January 2006
• Log and edit videotape
• Assist the sports anchor
• Research and write stories for on-air use

University Directories   South Bend, IN
Sales Representative   Summer 2005
• Used a variety of sales strategies to sell advertising
• Enhanced communication and organization skills
• Built rapport with local business owners

Robert Gill Builders   Rochester, MN
Carpenter   Summer 2001 - 2004
• Performed manual labor required to frame houses
• Developed a better understanding of the home-building industry
• Applied active listening techniques to ensure accuracy of projects

Activities: Milton Home, Volunteer, 2003
Bookstore Basketball, Participant, Spring 2002, 2003 & 2004
Cedar Rapids Rough Rider USHL Team, 2000-2002

Carolyn Nicole Neff

218 Breen-Phillips Hall
Notre Dame, IN 46556
(805) 233-2217
cneff@nd.edu

OBJECTIVE Obtain a full-time position in brand management.

EDUCATION **University of Notre Dame**, Notre Dame, IN
Bachelor of Business Administration, Marketing   May 2006
GPA: 3.1   Marketing GPA: 3.9

HONORS
Robert M. Satterfield Award	Fall 2005
Dean's List	Fall 2004
California Governor's Scholar Award	2001-2002
California Scholarship Federation Member	1999-2002

EXPERIENCE

Marketing **Countrywide Financial Corporation**, Westlake Village, CA
Corporate Marketing Intern   Summer, Winter 2005
- Created comprehensive presentation incorporating all aspects of major corporate sponsorship.
- Researched fraudulent domain name registration and detected infringements of company policies.
- Played integral role in planning convention to be attended by company executives.

Notre Dame Marketing Department, Notre Dame, IN
Teaching Assistant - Communicating Value-Based Solutions Spring 2006
- Plans in progress to rewrite and reformat course materials.

Teaching Assistant - Quantitative Analysis Course   2005-2006 Academic Year
- Host lab hours to assist students with data analysis software homework.

Amgen, Inc., Thousand Oaks, CA
Marketing Intern   Summer 2004
- Clerical work within marketing department.
- Job allowed for the expansion of communication and administrative skills in a corporate environment.

Sales
Gap, Inc., Camarillo, CA	Summer 2003
Just Sports, Camarillo, CA	Summer 2003
Starbucks, Notre Dame, IN	2003-2005

Sales Associate
- Gained significant experience working face-to-face with customers in retail environment.
- Used creative capacities to manipulate displays in an effort to leverage sales.

Customer Service **Hesburgh Library,** Notre Dame, IN
Microform Staff Clerk   Spring 2006

LEADERSHIP *Marketing Club President*   2004-2005 Academic Year
- Increased membership by 200% during term as president.
- Coordinated and oversaw many events, including recruitment presentations, fundraisers, competitions, and community service.

Hyatt Regency Sales Blitz Team Captain   Fall 2005
- Led team of 10 students in sales competition in Indianapolis.
- Coordinated all logistics and planning of trip, as well as weekly training sessions to prepare for competition.

Freshman Orientation Leader   Fall 2003
- Planned and led new student orientation for 80 freshmen in my dorm.

ACTIVITIES
Spring Visitation Week Host	2003-2005
Our Lady of Hungary – Tutoring Program	2005
There Are Children Here – Daycare Program	2005

CHARLES A. BASSETT, II
cbassett@nd.edu

Current Address:	Permanent Address:
1503 North Oakhill	11682 Garnsey Ave.
South Bend, IN 46637	Grand Haven, MI 49417
616-638-7960	616-846-2588

Objective   An entry-level management position in corporate finance

Education

University of Notre Dame   Notre Dame, IN
Bachelor of Business Administration   May 2006
Major: Finance   GPA: 3.56/4.00
          Major GPA: 3.72/4.00

Experience

Charles Bassett Properties, LLC, Grand Haven, MI
President   2004-Present
- Created investment partnership to hold income producing properties
- Continually search market for attractive properties
- Arrange appropriate financing for properties

Westcoast Property Management, LLC, Muskegon, MI
Vice President   2001-Present
- Analyze investment opportunities for partnership
- Arrange appropriate financing for properties

Pizahz, LLC, Grand Rapids, MI
Co-President   2004-Present
- Created business plan for new concept restaurant
- Team leader in strategic planning

AIM Fund, Notre Dame, IN
Analyst   Current
- Analyze 2 stock opportunities for multi-million dollar portfolio
- Continue 10 year tradition of earning 3+ basis points over the S&P 500

Med Services, Inc, Grand Rapids, MI
Consultant   2004-Present
- Develop strategic plans for existing and new business lines

Med-1, Inc, Holland, MI
Medical Technician   Summer 2002-2003
- Served as quasi-bilingual medical technician in occupational clinic

Leadership

Student Union Board, Notre Dame, IN
Director of Operations   2005-Present
- Co-ordinate and direct operations of 50+ person team, sit on Executive Board

Class Council, Notre Dame, IN
Representative   2002-2005

Campus and Academic Enrichment Committee, Notre Dame, IN
Chairman   2003-2005

Service

Memorial Hospital Pediatric ICU, South Bend, IN
Volunteer   2002-2003

CHRISTOPHER H. FINCH

424 N. FRANCIS STREET • APARTMENT 4 • SOUTH BEND, IN • 46617
970-471-5271 • CFINCH@ND.EDU

OBJECTIVE

To obtain a position as a financial analyst utilizing communication, leadership, and logic.

EDUCATION

UNIVERSITY OF NOTRE DAME Notre Dame, IN
Bachelor of Business Administration, May 2006
Concentration: Finance   GPA: 3.115   Major GPA: 3.4

EXPERIENCE

VAIL SECURITIES INVESTMENTS, INC. Vail, CO
Broker/Dealer and Securities Trader   Summer 2002/03/04
- Attained **Series 7 – Broker/Dealer** license.
- Dealt with clients and managed portfolios valuing up to $500,000.
- Traded and valued securities with both long term and short term focus (NASD, NYSE, OTC).
- Assisted with $9 Million private placement, ReGen Biologics.
- Day traded on speculation, technical analysis, and momentum.

DUNDEE REALTY CORP. (REIT) Toronto, ON
Property Management Analyst   Summer 2005
- Assisted in tenant lease negotiations and closings.
- Analyzed risk in leases and aided in producing forecasts of revenues and expenses.
- Developed a new database for efficiency in referencing mortgage contracts.

ACTIVITIES

Captain and Manager, Fisher Hall Intramural Soccer, 2004
Captain and Manager, Fisher Hall Intramural Ice Hockey, 2004
Captain, Fisher Hall Intramural Roller Hockey, 2003/04
Captain, Fisher Hall Intramural Floor Hockey, 2003/04
Boxer, Bengal Bouts Boxing Club, 2003/04
Volunteer, Robinson Community Learning Center, 2003/04
Lead Guitarist, Garage band with friends, 2002-Present
Speaker Repair Mechanic, Finch Speaker Repair/Replacement

HONORS

NSCAA Soccer All-American
Harvard University Scholar Award
National Milk/USA Today Scholarship Award
National Merit Scholar Semi-Finalist
Battle Mountain High School Outstanding Senior of 2002

Joseph M. McFarlane

Current Address:
18063 Bulla Rd. Apt B
South Bend, IN 46637
(574) 315-5343

jmcfarla@nd.edu

Permanent Address:
1502 Emery Street
Eau Claire, WI 54701
(715) 835-7518

OBJECTIVE

Obtain a position as a Business Management Associate with General Mills

EDUCATION

UNIVERSITY OF NOTRE DAME, Notre Dame, IN
Bachelor of Arts, Marketing, May 2006
GPA: 3.253/4.0

UNIVERSITY OF NOTRE DAME AUSTRALIA, Fremantle, Australia
Studied abroad in Fall 2004

HONORS

National Dean's List Honoree 2003-2004 Academic Year
International Business Certificate, University of Notre Dame, Fall 2004

EXPERIENCE

ACCION CHICAGO - Chicago, IL
Marketing Intern   Summer 2005
- Analyzed loan data
- Conducted market analysis and segmentation, database management
- Created various marketing research questionnaires
- Represented ACCION Chicago at conventions, expos, etc

HESBURGH LIBRARY - Notre Dame, IN
Student Assistant   Fall 2002 - Present
- Gained administrative experience and organizational tactics in a team atmosphere
- Data entry projects, self-paced goals

DECIO COMMONS - Notre Dame, IN
Student Assistant   Fall 2002 - Present
- Inventory management and customer relationship experience
- Decio is an on-campus deli for students and staff

SUMMER SERVICE INTERNSHIP - Oshkosh, WI & Milwaukee, WI
Summer Program Director   Summer 2004
- Worked in Oshkosh at a men's homeless shelter and free health clinic
- Helped to direct a youth summer program, including daily field trips throughout Milwaukee

STUDENT BODY PRESIDENT - Eau Claire, WI
Service Coordinator   2001-2002 Academic Year
- Planned and coordinated service activities for my high school

SKILLS

Computer: HTML, Dreamweaver, SPSS, PowerPoint, Word, Access, Excel, Publisher

ACTIVITIES

Center for Social Concerns – Summer Service Task Force – Publicity Director
Notre Dame Marketing Club - Member
Notre Dame Encounter – Assistant Coordinator
Camp Kesem – Counselor
Habitat for Humanity - Member
Intramural Sports (football, basketball, horseshoes) - Participant

Lataros C. Graves
lgraves@nd.edu

Permanent Address	College Campus Address
14501 Ingleside Ave.	218 Pasquerilla West Hall
Dolton, IL 60419	Notre Dame, IN 46556
(708) 201-1337	(574) 634-2966
Mobile: (708) 668-3542	

OBJECTIVE

Obtain an internship in investment banking for the summer of 2006

EDUCATION

University of Notre Dame   **Notre Dame, IN**
Bachelor of Business Administration   January 2007
Major: Finance
Major GPA: 3.89/4.0, Business GPA: 3.864/4.0, Cumulative GPA: 3.546/4.0
Dean's List: Fall 2005, Spring 2005, Fall 2004

Relevant Coursework
- Two Semesters of Finance: Essentials of Corporate Finance, Investment Theory
- Three Semesters of Accounting: Financial, Managerial, Measurements & Disclosures I
- Four Semesters of Economics: Micro, Macro, Managerial Economics, Intermediate Macro
- *2006 Spring Semester : Security Analysis, Advanced Corporate Finance*

EXPERIENCE

Summer 2005   **US Bank, Private Client Group/Commercial Banking Group**   **Chicago, IL**
INROADS *Intern*
- Pioneered a project that consolidated prospective client information and created a user-friendly database of this information
- Created an advisory board presentation for the President of the Chicago Market
- Coordinated all the event planning for meetings with clients and bankers
- Assisted commercial banking and private banking clients with everyday banking needs

Summer 2004   **US Bank, Private Client Group**   **Chicago, IL**
INROADS *Intern*
- Assisted Relationship Managers and Managing Director with daily tasks
- Aided clients with banking needs
- Coordinated various events, including sales meetings and conference calls
- Prepared presentations and data spreadsheets for the Managing Director

September 2003-   **University of Notre Dame, Athletic Department**   **Notre Dame, IN**
April 2004   *Student Athletic Trainer*
- Performed ultrasounds and electrical stem treatments
- Drove athletes to and from medical treatment sessions
- Helped train new student athletic trainers

December 2002-   **Wilson's Leather**   **Calumet City, IL**
August 2003   *Sales Associate*
- Was top sales associate 32 of 34 weeks of employment
- Achieved 100% of set goals every week of employment
- Earned employee of the month honor four of eight months employed

SKILLS

Proficient in Microsoft Excel, Word, PowerPoint, Access, and DreamWeaver

ACTIVITIES

- Harris Nesbitt Job Shadow Internship
- Student Union Assistant Treasurer
- PwC xTax Case Competiton
- Undergraduate Women in Business
- Investment Club
- Class of 2007 Council
- Urban Plunge Experience
- Shades of Ebony

LAUREN VINCENT CENTIOLI

121 Dillon Hall • Notre Dame, Indiana 46556 • 574.634.1593
144 Woodley Road • Winnetka, Illinois 60093 • 847.441.4558
847.977.6575 Cell • Email: centioli.1@nd.edu

EDUCATION

UNIVERSITY OF NOTRE DAME, Notre Dame, Indiana
Bachelor of Business Administration   January 2007
Accountancy   Anthropology Minor
GPA: 3.4/4.0   Major GPA: 3.9/4.0

HONORS

Dean's List
Beta Alpha Psi

EXPERIENCE

ICON LLC, Chicago, Illinois
Web Administrator   September 2005 – Present
Web Administrator/Postmaster   June 2004 – September 2005
Travel Coordinator   March 1999 – Present

- Responsible for acquisition and maintenance of 17 domain names, including icon.com and icon.ca
- Managed websites for parent company and 3 affiliates, including over 100 email accounts, and over 20 email lists
- Created and maintain internal administrative website
- Responsible for booking travel for CEO, COO and CFO

LETTUCE ENTERTAIN YOU ENTERPRISES, INC. & ICON LLC, Chicago, Illinois
Corporate Accounting Intern   Summer 2004, Summer 2005
Joe's Seafood, Prime Steak & Stone Crab Management Intern Summer 2005

- Created and revamped internal spreadsheets
- Staff accountant duties, including weekly and monthly reporting to Krispy Kreme Doughnuts, Inc. (NYSE: KKD).
- Assisted restaurant managers and maitre d' during all shifts
- Filled restaurant lunch maitre d' position during some shifts

KSMB ASSOCIATES, Glenview, Illinois
Web Administrator   Summer 2005 – Present
Accounting Assistant   Summer 2005

- Responsible for domain, email, and website (in-progress)
- Assisted in accounting duties for a small business client, mainly bookkeeping and records

ACTIVITIES

Aviation, *Federal Aviation Administration*   January 2001 – Present
- o   Commercial Pilot
- o   Certified Flight Instructor
- o   Advanced Ground Instructor

Instructor, *University of Notre Dame*   Fall 2004 – Present (4 semesters)
- o   AS30098 - Intro to Principles of Flight, 3.0 credit hours

Scuba Diving, *Professional Association of Diving Instructors* July 1998 – Present
- o   Advanced Open Water Diver
- o   Medic First Aid

Second Lieutenant – *Civil Air Patrol, USAF Auxiliary*
Participant – *Tax Assistance Program (VITA)*
Referee – *Illinois High School Association (IHSA) – Football*
Catechesis Assistant – *St. Pius X*
Volunteer/Site Leader – *Christian Outreach with Appalachian People*
Member – *Notre Dame Accounting Association*
Participant – *Deloitte Case Competition*
Participant – *Relay for Life*
Participant – *Notre Dame Intramural Athletics*

SKILLS

Computer: *Word, Excel, Access, PowerPoint, FrontPage, Dreamweaver*

Meghan Winger

Current Address: 54650 Willis St. • South Bend, IN • 46637 • (321) 947-0675 • mwinger@nd.edu
Permanent Address: 3012 Seigneury Dr. • Windermere, FL • 34786 • (407) 876-8665

OBJECTIVE

To obtain an entry-level management position in marketing

EDUCATION

UNIVERSITY OF NOTRE DAME, NOTRE DAME, IN
Bachelor of Business Administration, May 2006
Major: Business Marketing
Cumulative GPA: 3.668/4.0

UNIVERSITY OF NOTRE DAME AUSTRALIA, FREMANTLE, WA
One of 30 students selected to participate Fall 2004
Certificate in International Studies

HONORS

Dean's List, three out of six semesters
National Dean's List, Freshman and Sophomore Year

RELEVANT EXPERIENCE

LEGEND'S OF NOTRE DAME, Notre Dame, IN
Marketing Assistant for Nightclub   Spring 2005 - Present
- Design, coordinate, and implement weekly marketing campaigns, including advertisements, promotional activities, and press releases for performing artists that come to the University entertainment venue
- Utilize interpersonal, organizational, and problem-solving skills to manage the needs of performers from the time they arrive on campus to the time they depart

UNIVERSITY OF NOTRE DAME NEWS AND INFORMATION OFFICE, Notre Dame, IN
Intern   Fall 2005
- Write and edit press releases regarding important news relating to the University of Notre Dame, its faculty, and its students
- Research and compose feature stories for the News and Information Office's website

NANCY SELTZER & ASSOCIATES, PUBLIC RELATIONS, Los Angeles, CA
Intern   Summer 2005
- Assisted in day-to-day media client relation's projects
- Demonstrated interpersonal and problem solving skills when dealing with clients and client requests
- Drafted and edited memos/correspondences for clients and the media
- Gained valuable experience and knowledge of the inter-workings of a public relations firm

SHOPLAWNDALE MAGAZINE, Los Angeles, CA
Sales   Summer 2005
- Utilized skills of persuasion and communication to sell advertising space in the launch issue of ShopLawdale magazine

LEADERSHIP/ ACTIVITIES

President (Spring 2005)/*Member* (2003-Present), Troop ND Dance Team
Volunteer, Circle K (Kiwanis), 2002 - Present
Member, Marketing Club, 2003 - Present
Member, Notre Dame Dance Company, Spring 2005 - Present
Dance Commissioner, Walsh Hall, 2003 - 2004
Choreographer and Performer, Welsh Family Dance Show, 2004 and 2005
Volunteer, There Are Children Here Urban Program, 2002

ADDITIONAL EXPERIENCE

OBGYN ASSOCIATES   Orlando, Fl
Office Assistant   Summers 2001 - 2004

UNIVERSITY OF NOTRE DAME LEARNING CENTER   Notre Dame, IN
Calculus Tutor   2003 - 2004

SKILLS

Computer: Word, Access, Excel, PowerPoint, Dreamweaver, HTML

MICHAEL T. FERKOVIC

Current Address:
307 Alumni Hall
Notre Dame, IN 46556
mferkovi@nd.edu

Permanent Add
1058 Oakview
Highland Heights, OH 4
cell: (440)-781-

OBJECTIVE	To obtain a summer internship in the accounting field and applying effective communication skills, problem solving, and technical skills.

EDUCATION

UNIVERSITY OF NOTRE DAME   Notre Dame
Degree: Bachelor of Business Administration, Accountancy
Graduation-December 2006
Overall G.P.A.: 3.281
Plan to sit for the CPA exam following Notre Dame's M.S.A.Progam (audit track)

ST. IGNATIUS HIGH SCHOOL   Cleveland
1999-2003
Cumulative G.P.A.: 4.41 (weighted 4.0 scale)
Graduated in top 5% of class (class of 360)

RELEVANT COURSES

- Accounting Measurement and Disclosure I & II, Accounting for Decision Making and Contr Federal Taxation
- Business Law I & II, IT Management and Applications, Business Finance, Operations & Competitive Enterprise, Strategic Management, Corporate Conscience

EXPERIENCE
Employment

DELOITTE & TOUCHE, LLP   Summer 2005-2006   Cleveland,
Audit & Assurance Services Intern
Examined various companies' financial statements to determine their reliability
Loaned Executive to the United Way of Greater Cleveland
Organized and ran campaigns in the public sector

SS&G HEALTHCARE SERVICES   December 2004   Fairlawn
Database Manager, Healthcare Services Division
Designed and maintained databases of medical practices using Microsoft Access

MICELI'S DAIRY PRODUCTS   December 2003   Cleveland,
String Cheese Line
Stacked and organized pallets of string cheese for shipping

STONEWATER GOLF CLUB   Summer 2000-2004   Highland Heights,
Greens Staff
Maintained the golf course environment by mowing greens, raking bunkers, and clea streams, lakes, and wetlands
Caddie
Worked various member tournaments at StoneWater and Mayfield C.C. in addition to normal caddie loops

Leadership & Scholarship Activities

UNIVERSITY OF NOTRE DAME
- Alumni Hall: Dorm President (2005-06), Freshmen Orientation Commissioner (2004), Merchandise Commissioner (2004-05), Retreat leader (2005), Intramural Sports (soccer, basketball) (2003-2006)
- Notre Dame Accounting Association

ST. IGNATIUS HIGH SCHOOL
- Treasurer of Student Senate, The Eye Newspaper Editor, Flag Football Tournament Founder Director to fight leukemia, Entrepreneurs' Club
- National Merit Commended Student, National Honor Society, First Honors each semester
- Division I Varsity Soccer Team (2001-2003), Cleveland United Soccer Club (1999-2003)

SKILLS   Intermediate and advanced level HTML, PowerPoint, Word, Access, and Excel

APPENDIX D

Graduate Resumes

Michael J. Daly
920 Saratoga Drive
West Chester, PA 19380
(484) 431-7983
Email: mdaly2@nd.edu

Objective: To obtain an institutional sales position with a leading firm that utilizes my dynamic business skills and leadership qualities as well as challenges me to continuously learn and contribute.

Education:

University of Notre Dame, South Bend, IN; May 2006
Masters of Business Administration

Villanova University, Villanova, PA; May 2000
Bachelor of Science in Business Administration
Major: Finance

Association of Investment Management and Research
Chartered Financial Analyst Level II Candidate

American College, Bryn Mawr, PA
Completed two self-study courses towards the Certified Financial Planner Designation.

Experience:

Brandywine Asset Management, LLC, Wilmington, DE
Summer Associate, May 2005 to Aug. 2005
- Develop Value-added presentations for consultant seminars and pension review boards.
- Implement strategy to improve internal sales structure.

Tower Bridge Advisors, West Conshohocken, PA
Investment Officer; Oct. 2001 to Aug. 2004
- Manage all private client and institutional marketing, including all RFP's and product inquiries from managers, consultants and trust officers.
- Develop and monitor equity research tools for use in analysis of model portfolio, equity recommendations and development of investment policies.
- Maintain client relationships and meet with clients on an on-going basis to review account.
- Head trader for all equity and fixed income accounts.

The Vanguard Group, Inc., Malvern, PA
Retirement Specialist; May 2000 to Oct. 2001
- Extensive marketing experience with High Net Worth individuals utilizing both face-to-face presentations and telephone conversations to capture assets.
- Identify and attempt to capture additional client assets through open dialogue.
- Recommend specific Vanguard mutual funds to fit investors' needs.
- Develop retirement plan models for High Net Worth shareholders.

School Inc., South Bend, IN
- Tutor/Mentor and Program liaison between elementary school and Notre Dame.

Archbishop John Carroll High School, Radnor, PA
- Head Freshman Boys Basketball Coach; October 1997 to October 2003.

Professional Licenses:
- **Series 6:** Investment Company/ Variable Contract Products Registered Representative.
- **Series 63:** Uniform Securities Registered State Representative.

Special Skills: Proficient in ACT!, Bloomberg, Baseline, Beta, Mobius, Security APL, and Microsoft Office.

Andre D. Bonakdar

1520 Marigold Way #609 • South Bend, IN 46617
abonakda@gmail.com • 574.876.3166 • 610.574.8324

EDUCATION	**UNIVERSITY OF NOTRE DAME**	Notre Dame, IN

Mendoza College of Business
Master of Business Administration, December 2005
- Emphases in Finance and General Management

	NAVAL NUCLEAR POWER PROGRAM	Charleston , SC

Master of Engineering Equivalent, Nuclear Engineering, June 1999
- Graduated in top 25% of the most academically challenging program in the Navy

	UNITED STATES NAVAL ACADEMY	Annapolis, MD

Bachelor of Science with Merit; Systems Engineering; May 1998
- Member of Tau Beta Pi and Golden Key National Honor Society for Engineering achievement
- Phi Alpha Theta Honor Society for excellence in History

EXPERIENCE **2003-Present**	**OFFICER EDUCATION PROGRAM; NOTRE DAME**	Notre Dame, IN

Assistant Professor of Naval Science
- Advised and mentored more than 100 undergraduate and graduate students providing personal development counseling and professional skills training
- Managed departmental IT networks including hardware acquisitions and security administration providing increased productivity and service for internal and external customers
- Achieved highest possible teacher evaluations due to innovative approach to traditional curriculum and cultivation of diverse student talents
- Developed innovative marketing strategy for officer scholarship program utilizing direct communication, advertising and database management. This coupled with excellent sales skills enabled the unit to meet all recruiting goals
- Recognized by departmental chairman as the most productive staff member due to leadership traits and contributions towards organizational success, and thus was nominated for national Naval Instructor of the Year

1998-2003	**US NAVY SURFACE WARFARE OFFICER**	San Diego, CA

Division Manager
- Consistently rated as top division officer among 16 peers and recommended for early promotion by the Commanding Officer for superior leadership and managerial skills
- Managed 54 people and $1.6 million budget during integrated training schedule prior to Persian Gulf deployment and during Operation Iraqi Freedom
- Named the top engineering officer out of 16 peers by a team of outside inspectors while leading a team of technicians during demanding simulated reactor casualties
- Selected by Department Head to lead cross functional certification and maintenance team during $4.2 billion nuclear aircraft carrier refueling
- Identified low morale situation within division and responded by developing a mentoring program for junior personnel. Realized 33% increase in retention; a major organizational objective and cost saving measure for the Navy
- Selected by department head as Departmental Training Officer for superior technical expertise, personality, and outstanding oral and written communication skills

ADDITIONAL INFORMATION
- Top Secret Clearance
- Recruited to play football and baseball at the Naval Academy

ANDREW J. FOWLER

5803 Sterling Dr, Apt 10
Granger, IN 46530
(770) 654-7088
afowler@nd.edu

Education

University of Notre Dame
Master of Business Administration
- Co-Chair of Academic and Student Affairs Committee
- GMAT 790

Notre Dame, IN
May 2006

Georgia Institute of Technology
Master of Science in Industrial Engineering

Atlanta, GA
December 2001

Georgia Institute of Technology
Bachelor of Industrial Engineering
- Minor in Industrial / Organizational Psychology
- Studied abroad at Oxford University in summer 1998

Atlanta, GA
June 1999

Experience

BellSouth Corporation
Industrial Engineer

Atlanta, GA
2001 - 2005

- Developed and maintained workforce sizing models to determine headcount needs for department of 3000+ employees
- Served as project manager for numerous time studies involving staff and center personnel of all job levels (standard times set for over 1000 activities)
- Managed implementation of process changes across 30 technical centers
- Reduced departmental budget by $150 million through process improvements and headcount reductions
- Worked closely with finance and marketing departments to develop forecasting tool
- Produced various measurement reports for all centers

Process Manager, Human Resources

2000 - 2001

- Streamlined employment testing process and reduced costs through increased use of mechanization
- Developed blueprint for strategically placing testing centers across southeastern United States to reduce travel expenses while minimizing additional headcount

Staffing Manager, Human Resources

1999 - 2000

- Staffed and managed cooperative education program
- Staffed and managed internship program
- Developed database to track student hires from initial work assignment to graduation
- Developed excellent communication skills through company presentations and student interviews on college campuses

Honors

- BellSouth's Gateway2 leadership program – limited to top 1% of employees
- Pinnacle Club Award – highest honor given at BellSouth
- University of Notre Dame Fellowship

ANGEL MARTIN LARGO
18285 Dunn Road
South Bend, IN 46637
(574) 323-6316
Angel.MartinLargo.1@nd.edu

Education

Notre Dame Business School   Notre Dame, IN
MBA   August 2004 - May 2006
- MBA Association Executive Council, Secretary
- Business & Technology Club, Corporate Development Director
- Marketing Club, member
- MBA Soccer Club, Founder and President
- Recipient of Notre Dame MBA Scholarship

Universidad Autonoma de Madrid   Madrid, Spain
Computer Engineering   September 1995 - September 1999
- Received merit based Government Scholarship, 100% of tuition and material

Experience

Valassis   Livonia, MI
$1 billion marketing services company listed as one of Fortune magazine's "Best Companies to Work For" for eight consecutive years.
New Business Development Intern   May 2005 - August 2005
- Supported senior leadership in developing a long-term strategy for growth. New strategy supported a vision that marked a dramatic change in corporate direction. Identified and evaluated:
  - Key consumer, media, and technology trends relating to vision
  - Key client pain points and trends by client segment
  - Potential partners and competitors
- Evaluated existing Internet-based consumer solutions, the gaps in their capability and ways to aggregate and improve upon existing solutions
- Competitive analysis including an evaluation of revenues, capabilities and consumer penetration

Hewlett Packard   Madrid, Spain
Computer products and services company, more than 140,000 employees
Solutions Manager   June 2000 - July 2004
- Solutions Manager:
  - Gathered and analyzed information from IT Call Center workflows in clients
  - Increased business volume of HP Solutions
  - Participated in the creation and design of a new department in the European region
  - Monitored the development of new products to match customer needs
- Project Manager:
  - Marketed new HP Solutions to enhance limited resources and solve customer needs
  - Led a team with members from different companies and countries
  - Succeeded in the design and implementation of a pioneer help desk solution
  - Received a "HP Customer Quality Recognition Award"
- Account Support Engineer:
  - Trained and supervised engineers from HP partners to deliver HP services
  - Achieved Microsoft Certified Systems Engineer (MCSE) certification

Up & Running Support Services   Madrid, Spain
Hewlett Packard Partner and Microsoft Solution Provider, more than 50 employees
Support Engineer   September 1998 - June 2000
- Researched, monitored, and solved Microsoft software incidents for HP clients

Personal

- Fluent in Spanish and English, intermediate fluency in French
- Special interest in innovation and new technologies

BECKY BANKOFF

5611 Sterling Drive Apt #12
Granger, IN 46530
404-931-5906
beckybankoff@hotmail.com

Education

University of Notre Dame - Mendoza College of Business   Notre Dame, IN
Master of Business Administration   May 2006
- Orientation Chair for incoming class of 2007
- MBA Open House 2004 Co-Chair and Student Ambassador
- Marketing Club, Merchandising Committee
- Women in Business, Activities Director

Emory University   Atlanta, GA
Bachelor of Arts in Sociology and Educational Studies   May 2000
- Emory University Honor Council Member
- Study Abroad, University College, London, England
- Varsity Volleyball, Co-captain

Experience

BP Lubricants, USA   Wayne, NJ
Brand Management Intern   May 2005 - August 2005
- Developed five variant concepts for SYNTEC, $40 million dollar motor oil brand. Analyzed market and competition, created appropriate consumer offers, evaluated consumer research, and presented recommendation to upper level management for consideration in 2006 brand plan.
- Variant recommendation for hybrid motor oil was approved and will go to test market in U.S.
- Analyzed current industry trends and simplified into overall business challenge of commoditization. Researched possible solutions and presented two in-depth resolutions to marketing management team.
- Led SYNTEC Scholarship Program which grew by 58% in its second year. Conducted weekly teleconference with Ogilvy Public Relations, coordinated website and newsletter promotions, assisted with entry and judging process, and facilitated the formation of media alerts, event materials, and press releases.
- Assisted in development of second half 2005 campaign including tv, print, and radio advertisements.
- Wrote BP Lubricants Business Case for Ogilvy & Mather and presented case and solution to their summer interns.

Cobb Galleria Centre   Atlanta, GA
National Sales Manager   2001 - 2004
- Managed direct sales efforts for national and regional conventions, tradeshows, and other events that resulted in $2.66 million in sales revenue or thirty percent of the annual operating budget. It was also the largest annual sales revenue amount in 10 year facility history.
- Secured contracts through the development of a network with Atlanta based franchise organizations, private companies, and Fortune 500 companies including The Home Depot, Bellsouth, and Cingular Wireless. Also contracted with governmental agencies including the Department of Education, Department of Homeland Security, and the White House.
- Negotiated complex contract language requested by clients to the Centre's Lease Agreement.
- Made sales visits and presentations to potential clients both locally and nationally at industry events and association tradeshows.
- Co-chaired Centre's team for the US 10K Classic benefiting the World's Children Center.

Activities

2005 - 2006: Notre Dame Women's Boxing Club
2004 - 2005: Youth Leadership Programming Committee, St. Joe County Chamber of Commerce
2002 - 2004: Atlanta Lawn and Tennis Association Co-Captain and city champion
2001 - current: Surfing in Australia, California, and New Jersey

BRYAN ANDREW SAUER
712 Travers Circle
Mishawaka, IN 46545
(616) 821-9694
bsauer@nd.edu

Education

University of Notre Dame - Mendoza College of Business South Bend, IN
Master of Business Administration May 2006
- Notre Dame MBA Fellowship Recipient
- GPA: 3.89

University of Delaware Newark, DE
Bachelor of Chemical Engineering 1999
- Science and Engineering Scholar
- Minors: Math, Chemistry

Experience

Ford Motor Company Dearborn, MI
Finance Intern 2005
- Developed, piloted, and deployed project to all 40+ Ford NA Manufacturing plants for estimated 41% reduction in the total value of NA Manufacturing unauthorized commitments.
- Achieved management consensus to deploy same project to all Ford Divisions.
- Identified root causal factors of unauthorized commitments using Six Sigma methodology.
- Coordinated monthly investigation and reporting at 40+ NA manufacturing plants for SOX compliance on unauthorized commitments and reported out to senior management.
- Developed standards and procedures to streamline and enhance investigation processes.
- Supported account reconciliations, special investigations, and plant audits.
- Ford Six Sigma Greenbelt Trained and Certified.

Pfizer Holland, MI
Automation Engineer 2001 – 2004
- Lead automation engineer on over $10MM in facility upgrade projects in 2004.
- Successfully led a time-critical $750K project to renovate, reprogram, and qualify a Rosenmund Filter/Dryer. Set expectations with managements, developed group consensus on project issues, and drove project to completion.
- Proposed and managed $600K in process upgrades. Achieved scope consensus with diverse customer base, attained approval from plant management, and executed project plan.
- Contributed as core team member for Gemfibrozil Process Improvement Team to evaluate and reduce variation in product manufacturing using Six Sigma and Kepner Trego tools.
- Delivered consistently excellent service through understanding of internal customer needs.

Applied Control Engineering Wilmington, DE
Sales Engineer 2000 – 2001
- Identified customer needs and selling points through personal involvement with target companies.
- Developed customers' financial justification through revenue generation and cost reduction models.
- Established preliminary system design, hardware, and software specifications for cost estimates.
- Managed and generated half of $2MM/month of project proposals.

Process Control Engineer
- Managed and performed renovation of manufacturing site in the plastics industry. Took an existing facility from operating in a completely manual fashion to utilizing a fully automated recipe management system.

Activities

- Lead Analyst – MBA Finance Club
- Treasurer – MBA Biotechnology and Healthcare Club
- West Michigan Masters Swim Team – Grand Rapids, MI

Graham A.R. McNally

gmcnally@nd.edu

1803 Corby Blvd.
South Bend, IN 46617
(H) (574)288-5591

109 Woodley Road
Winnetka, IL 60093
(C) (847)624-7971

EDUCATION	**Notre Dame Law School**, South Bend, IN. Candidate for JD degree (expected 2006) GPA: 3.0/4.0 **Brown University**, Providence, RI. BA degree: May 2002 **Major:** Economics Overall GPA: 3.5/4.0 Senior Year GPA: 4.0/4.0 NCAA Division I Hockey Goaltender (1998-2000)
WORK EXPERIENCE	**Medical Business Associates**, Chicago, IL. **Summer 2005** Intern • Researched and prepared memoranda re: heightening recognition and improving prevention of fraud in the workplace • Researched similar art pertaining to an impending patent **American Cancer Society**, Chicago, IL. **Summer 2004** Intern • Assisted with distinguished giving legal affairs in the Illinois Division • Headed various legal, fundraising, marketing, and business development projects with a focus on strengthening the involvement of young adults **Vedder, Price, Kaufman, & Kammholz**, Chicago, IL **Summer 2003** Intern • Assisted with research, analysis, and document preparation in various practice areas including Exec Compensation, Capital Markets, & Insurance Coverage Litigation **Universal Music Group**, Los Angeles, CA. **Summer 2001** Intern • Assisted in start-up of Universal's music/writing eLearning venture, InsideSessions, by researching and preparing analysis for partnership opportunities/competitors and assisting in "grass roots" marketing • Assisted in Promotion, Marketing & New Media departments at Universal's Interscope A&M Records label **Mission Hockey** (equipment company), Santa Ana, CA. **Summers 2000-01** Brand Activator • Represented and promoted Mission Hockey at domestic and international roller and ice hockey events in Florida, Nevada, and California • Supported individual athlete and team services **Minnesota Wild** (National Hockey League), Minneapolis/St. Paul, MN. **Summer 1999** Intern • Assisted in start-up of new NHL franchise, promoted the Minnesota Wild brand, and helped the Wild achieve the 4th highest season ticket sales of the 30 NHL franchises **Chapman & Cutler,** Chicago, IL. **Summer 1998** Intern • Assisted in various practice areas including mergers & acquisitions, loan documentation, closings, and collections **Rick Heinz Goalie Schools**, Chicago, IL. **Summers 1994-97** Hockey Instructor/Counselor
SKILLS & INTERESTS	Interests include golf, tennis, and cooking Head Hockey Coach for the Rhode Island School of Design Club Hockey Team (2001-02)

ISABELLE ANNE COTE
1115 Oak Ridge Street
South Bend, IN 46617
206 949-9682
icote@nd.edu

Education

University of Notre Dame — Notre Dame, IN — May 2006
Masters in Business Administration (MBA)
- Concentration: Marketing and Management Development
- Notre Dame MBA Fellowship recipient
- Marketing Club - VP Operations and Director of Merchandising,
- Admission Interviewer, Student Ambassador, Co-chair for the Red Cross Blood Drive

McGill University — Montreal, Canada — May 2002
Bachelor of Commerce
- Accounting and Marketing concentrations

Experience

South Africa Internship Program — Cape Town, South Africa — 2005
Intern
- Advised Community Creations, a division of Ikamva Labantu (a local non-governmental, not for profit organization)
- Explored US export opportunities of arts and crafts through product development, market research, and merchandising

BMO Investorline — Montreal, Canada
Brokerage firm and financial services
Client Services Associate — 2003-2004
- Processed stock market transactions, offered diverse financial services and products to clients, advised clients of stock reorganizations, successfully improved response time to clients' requests from 48 to 24 hours

JYPCO Inc. — Montreal, Canada
Real estate
Market Research Coordinator — 2003 - 6 month contract
- Gathered and analyzed data for all residential markets where the company is involved in the Montreal Area, made recommendations for future investments

Chubb Insurance Company of Canada — Montreal, Canada
Underwriter, Commercial Insurance Specialty — 2002-2003
- Analyzed new account submissions and decided whether to insure these companies and under what conditions, managed the book of business for all Quebec city brokers, increased new business and renewal premiums by 25%
- Top 10 in a class of over 100 trainees at Chubb Specialty School in Warren, New Jersey

National Bank of Canada — Montreal, Canada
Customer Service Representative — 2000-2002

Activities and Sports

- Volunteer: Manoir de l'Age d'Or (residence for elders), 2003
- President of Social Committee: Chubb Insurance Company of Canada, 2002-2003
- Class President (Senior year): Pensionnat du Saint-Nom-de-Marie (Secondary School), 1997
- Canadian Windsurfing team member from 1992 to 1997, represented Canada for the World Youth Sailing Championship in Fukuoka, Japan

Languages

- Fluent in French and English, Basic Spanish

KATE E. MCHUGH

1242 White Oak Drive • South Bend, Indiana 46617
617.549.2655 • kmchugh1@nd.edu

OBJECTIVE

Apply my proven analytical and negotiation skills to merchandising for a major fashion retailer.

EDUCATION

UNIVERSITY OF NOTRE DAME – MENDOZA COLLEGE OF BUSINESS   NOTRE DAME, IN
Master of Business Administration – Marketing   Expected Graduation: May 2006
Marketing club (Merchandising Committee), Admissions Interviewer, Honor Code Review Committee
GPA: 3.85

COLLEGE OF THE HOLY CROSS   WORCESTER, MA
Bachelor of Arts- Spanish/Economics   May 2000
GPA: 3.5, Varsity Crew

UNIVERSITY OF THE BALEARIC ISLANDS   PALMA DE MAJORCA, SPAIN
All coursework conducted in Spanish   August 1998-May 1999
Independent Projects: Spanish Fashion Study, Integration of the Euro in Majorca

PROFESSIONAL EXPERIENCE

PRICEWATERHOUSECOOPERS, L.L.P. (PwC)   BOSTON, MA
C.P.A., Senior Audit Associate   June 2000 – July 2004
- Led cross-functional team conducting audits of public company financial statements
- Performed financial analysis and due diligence for IPOS and business acquisitions
- Negotiated project fees with client senior management
- Designed marketing materials and proposals which led to audit and consulting contracts of $200,000
- Managed and coached 25 associates on 10 different client engagements
- Served as key client account contact on a daily basis, interacting will all levels of clients' business
- Prepared analytics on economics of specific projects in order to improve team member utilization by 15%
- Promoted to senior position ahead of a majority of start class

PwC ENTREPRENEURIAL SERVICES CENTER   BOSTON, MA
Research Analyst   Summer 2003
- Edited business plans and assessed financial forecasts of new and experienced entrepreneurs, securing funding for two start-ups during a three month period

INDIANA VENTURE CENTER   INDIANAPOLIS, IN
Strategy Consultant   Summer 2005
- Provided management and marketing consulting to potential high-growth, high-tech companies in Indiana
- Developed marketing plan for the RCA tennis tournament which led to increased sales from prior year

RELEVANT SKILLS
- Advanced Excel, PowerPoint, SPSS, SalesLogix (CRM database management)
- Proficient in the Spanish language
- Recreational designer (stationary, handbags and accessories)

KIMBERLY ANN LONG
303-2A Runaway Bay Circle
Mishawaka, IN 46545
214-417-3443
klong4@nd.edu

Education

University of Notre Dame   Notre Dame, IN
Master of Business Administration, Concentration: Corporate Finance & Consulting   May 2006
- Class of 2006 Representative, MBA Association- Student Government
- Consulting Club, Finance and Investment Club, Net Impact, Women in Business

Texas Tech University   Lubbock, TX
Bachelor of Business Administration, Finance & Economics   May 2000
- Golden Key National Honor Society, Cardinal Key National Honor Society, Finance Association, Marketing Association, Alpha Phi Sorority

Experience

JPMorgan Chase   Dallas, TX
Senior Corporate Trust Analyst   March 2004 – May 2005
- Manage client portfolio with over 2k accounts by assisting Relationship Manager on all aspects of new and existing municipal debt deals
- Monitor bond deal activities including structuring, refunding, escrow investments and call redemption
- Work closely with external clients, underwriters, financial advisors, rating agencies and bond counsels to close new deals and resolve client inquiries before and after deal closings
- Involved in several Six Sigma projects to ensure smooth transition of Bank One clients and systems to JPMorgan platforms post-merger

Senior Operations Analyst, Team Lead   April 2002 – March 2004
- Promoted to Lead position after 15 months with team
- Developed first income generating process for securities settlement division
- Assisted manager in all training, development, and motivation of eight-member team
- Analyzed general ledger to determine and resolve discrepancies between internal and external accounting trade systems to recover clients assets

Securities Specialist   October 2000 – March 2002
- Crucial member of original team hired to successfully transfer all Securities Settlement operations from New York to Dallas prior to JPMorgan and Chase Manhattan merger
- Responsible for settlement of all internal accounts that trade through the Depository Trust Company (DTC) and the National Securities Clearing Corporation (NSCC)
- Appropriated DTC and NSCC Net Settlement cash funds to over 80 client accounts daily with average value between $50 million to $1.2 billion per account

Southwest Corporate   Dallas, TX
Investment Credit Analyst   June 2000 – September 2000
- Analyzed firm's investment portfolio with assets totaling over $4 billion, including analysis of individual security performances, projections for all investments, and credit worthiness
- Gathered quarterly and annual financial statements for a variety of firms invested in, creating extensive Excel spreadsheets to analyze credit strength
- Compiled credit reports for senior management and members of Board of Directors using above research and analysis

Morgan Stanley   Lubbock, TX
Intern   April 1999 – September 1999
- Worked directly for Senior VP responsible for High Net Worth Retirement Portfolios
- Participated in a variety of brokerage activities including cold-calling, client database creation, new venture stock offerings, and pitches

LAURA C. HANLEY
27 Fischer Grad Res Apt 1A
Notre Dame, Indiana 46556
574-634-4469
lhanley@nd.edu

Education

University of Notre Dame   Notre Dame, Indiana
Master of Business Administration   May 2006
- Notre Dame MBA Fellowship Recipient
- Chair, School Inc. Committee
- Secretary, Graduate Women in Business
- Six Sigma Green Belt Preparation

The George Washington University   Washington, D.C.
B.A., International Affairs   May 1999

Experience

South Africa Internship Program

Cape Town, South Africa
2005
- Coordinated independent evaluation of Ikamva Labantu's childcare training program. Monitored and assisted independent evaluators and reported progress to Ikamva staff. Recommended changes to evaluation process to better track cultural changes among childcare workers in townships
- Facilitated competitive and customer analysis for 5 in 6 Trust. Developed corporate fundraising strategy based on analysis and research on South African corporate citizenship. Consulted on new communications strategy

American School Food Service Association   Alexandria, Virginia
Senior New Media Specialist   2000-2004
- Enhanced ASFSA's voice through its Web site (www.asfsa.org), e-newsletters and additional electronic communications. Increased average monthly site visits by 60%
- Identified audience interests and needs and managed development of appropriate content. Tripled average number of front-page news stories that appeared each month
- Determined best delivery options for content. Introduced e-newsletters and online chats as new distribution vehicles. E-newsletter subscription base increased to 4500 individuals in one year
- Led and participated in inter-departmental teams. Involved at all stages of project development for interactive site tools, from idea creation to promotion and marketing. Managed vendor relationships and production schedules
- Travelled to provide Web site training to members with varying degrees of computer skill. Trained co-workers on use of office intranet and Web site
- Chaired Knowledge Management team. Developed ASFSA knowledge management pledge

Foundation Specialist   1999-2000
- Promoted to Foundation Specialist after serving as Operations Administrator, Foundation and Knowledge Center, for eight months. Promoted to Operation Administrator after six months as Foundation Assistant
- Wrote monthly reports to major donors. Generated monthly invoices and acknowledgements. Consolidated donor files to better track donors' involvement in multiple giving programs
- Developed Web sponsorships package valued at over $150,000
- Assisted in planning and execution of annual silent auction and golf tournament benefits
- Liaison to the Foundation Board and an advisory committee of the ASFSA Executive Board. Served as information resource for volunteer leadership and coordinated meetings

Awards and Activities

- ASFSA Outstanding Staff Achievement Award (2002), APEX Award for Excellence for One to Two Person-Produced Web & Intranet Sites (2004), ASAE Gold Circle Award - Web site category (2000)
- Coordinator of Platinum and Gold Award-winning United Way Campaigns (1999-2004)
- Personal Interests. Community service, working with children, children's literature

8 FISCHER GRADUATE RESIDENCES APT 1-A • NOTRE DAME, IN 46556
PHONE (555) 555-5555 • EMAIL MKIMMET@ND.EDU

MARK J. KIMMET

EDUCATION

University of Notre Dame Mendoza College of Business Notre Dame, IN
Masters in Business Administration Candidate May 2006

- Concentration in Consulting and Information Technology
- First Place Winner of the 2005 IBM Notre Dame Case Competition
- GPA 3.71, GMAT 720 (96 Percentile)

University of Notre Dame Notre Dame, IN
Bachelor of Business Administration, Management Information Systems January 2003

- Graduated Magna Cum Laude, 3.778 GPA

EXPERIENCE

University of Notre Dame Mendoza College of Business Notre Dame, IN
Systems Engineer, Mendoza Information Technology Jan. 2003 – May 2005

- Responsible for maintenance and backup of 10 application, web, and streaming video servers
- Wrote more than 50 technology tutorials and documents for faculty and staff
- Trained staff in new software and provided support
- Advised college departments on new technology and software implementation
- Implemented disaster recovery and backup plan for college systems and data
- Conducted security planning for college servers and data
- Created web applications and maintained the Mendoza Information Technology website

Student Web and Database Developer, Mendoza Information Technology Jan. 2001 – Dec. 2002

- Launched and maintained the Mendoza Information Technology website
- Designed and implemented online Knowledge Base for faculty and staff technology questions
- Created web based content management system for easy modification of department website
- Developed online web database applications and surveys for faculty and staff

Private Part-Time Consulting South Bend, IN
2001 – 2004

- Created an invoice and bookkeeping application that integrated with a point of sales system to allow for finance charges on overdue balances, and to print over 2,000 invoices a month
- Oversaw and developed a dynamic data entry and fulfillment application for entry and printing of 40,000 rebate letters for a local fulfillment company

PROFESSIONAL SKILLS

- Proficient in programming JavaScript, Coldfusion, SQL, HTML, CSS, PHP, C++

ACTIVITIES & INTERESTS

- Volunteer at the Logan Center for people with disabilities
- Co-Chair of MBA Association Communication Committee
- Triathlons, Running, Mountaineering, Photography, Reading, Creating Websites